STUFF

PEOPLE MIGHT WANT TO KNOW

To: BRIAN
" DOUBLE B "
BAUER

From the MORNING
BREAK AND BEYOND...

Hope u ENJOY

(COACH)

STUFF

PEOPLE MIGHT WANT TO KNOW

FROM SOMEONE WHO REALLY SHOULDN'T BE WRITING A BOOK

A Book of Lighthearted Observations, Opinions, and Essays—
with Some Deep Thoughts Thrown In Just for Laughs

Written by

Jon "Coach" Cohn

Longtime Reader…First-Time Writer

STUFF PEOPLE MIGHT WANT TO KNOW
From Someone Who Really Shouldn't Be Writing a Book

Windy City Publishers
2118 Plum Grove Road, #349
Rolling Meadows, IL 60008

www.windycitypublishers.com

Published in the United States of America

ISBN#:
978-1-941478-24-0

Library of Congress Control Number:
2016931827

WINDY CITY PUBLISHERS
CHICAGO

Dedicated to:

Hmmm...

How about to the grandchildren I do not yet have.
(No pressure, Kevin and David—take your time!)

Just in case I am not around, this book will at least let them know
the strange thoughts and weird ideas
(and hopefully understand the deep heart)
their grandpa had.

Also dedicated to:
The many who laughed, ignored, or politely smiled
when told I was writing a book—
and who didn't really think I would finish it.
Thank you.

Whenever I got stuck or didn't think I could do any more...
I just pushed through thinking of you.

More Dedication...

Profits from this book will go in part to the following
charitable organizations:

Connections for the Homeless
An organization dedicated to assisting the homeless in all areas
from housing to counseling to health and social services.
www.cfthinc.org

Dreams for Kids
An organization begun by the amazing Tom Touhy
(the organization's story is beautifully depicted in the book *Kiss of a Dolphin*)
dedicated to serving underprivileged and challenged children and families
both in this country and abroad. Their annual Holiday Party, held in
different states and in different countries throughout the world,
is one of the largest such charitable functions.
www.dreamsforkids.org

Juvenile Protective Association
A Chicago-based organization begun by Jane Addams back in 1901.
Provides assistance, counseling, education,
and other support programs to families in need.
www.juvenile.org

Special Olympics
A longtime organization dedicated to providing sports, physical activities,
and competition for those with mental and/or physical challenges.
www.specialolympics.org

About the Author...

Cohn is fifty-nine years old,
and this is his first time writing a book.

But enough about him…

Foreword By????

We are leaving this space open right now. All options are on the table. Not sure anyone has earned the right yet for this not-so-prestigious honor, but we are open to suggestions.

In fact, we are wide open.

After the first publication of this book (optimistically thinking it actually gets that far), if any of our fine readers are moved enough to want to write a foreword for the next publication, well, that would be great! You're on!

If we get a bunch of good ones, I am even open to multiple forewords. What the heck… I might even put a foreword at the end of the book. Maybe even in the middle, just to sort of break up the monotony, if you know what I mean. Whatever works.

If you want to move "foreword," email us at: jcsportsandtees@aol.com and we will go from there.

This could be your big break in journalism…or it could be a nice project for, say, a fourth-grade writing class. At any rate, I am leaving the options open for you, the reader, to write the foreword to this book.

Such excitement. Imagine the possibilities!

Some Friendly STUFF Reminders before the Ready, Set, Read!

The opinions expressed in this book are not necessarily the opinions of the editors or publishers of this book. Definitely not. In fact, in all likelihood, they could be quite the opposite.

This book is meant to be interactive and will serve as a jumping-off point for our website and possible blog page. We encourage you to comment on any part of the book and offer thoughts and suggestions, etc. They will be shared at our official STUFF website (coming soon). For all comments, or to get on to our mailing list, contact our email address at jcsportsandtees@aol.com.

Much thanks to the inventors and creators of spell-check, without which this original manuscript would have otherwise been unreadable and illegible. (Possibly illegal?)

If you are a wedding planner, tax professional, consultant, commodities trader, or lobbyist, 1) I apologize in advance. Nothing personal. 2) Be forewarned, 3) Always remember to keep your sense of humor, and 4) If you Google or research a fact-finding website, and find my actual home address, sorry, but I have moved.

Final reminder as you enter these pages, to begin a journey of admittedly unforeseen outcomes—we offer to you the following words of advice:

Always remember…your seat cushion may be used as a flotation device—and more importantly…

"He who laughs, lasts."

And now...

In no particular order...
(by the way, this was the second choice for the book title)

Let's get to some STUFF!

Reminder...

For all comments on book items AND to be informed on
the upcoming STUFF website, please email us at
jcsportsandtees@aol.com.

The First Item

Wow. Item number one. In a book of items printed in no particular order...

So much pressure on that lead-off topic....

Nobody wants to go first. Being first means you are the guinea pig everyone else learns from. It is like diving from a high bridge into the water below, hoping there are no rocks and that it is deep enough.

Then again, when you go first, you get it over with first. You can then sit back and watch everyone else suffer.

Remember, this book is going to be a random collection of opinions, suggestions, observations, and occasionally an offered solution. So how do you pick which one goes first? Do you start with the most important and then work down? Do you start with a teaser? Do you start with a trivial item, and then work your way up to a blistering crescendo? So many decisions? So few answers...so much pressure on what to put first...

Pause. Strategic delay.

Good, I think we filled (killed?) enough space to complete item number one.

Whew! Now the pressure is off. Let's move on to the rest of the book.

Silence in the Dentist's Office!

Okay, we all know we have to go in for some dreaded dental work at some point. It's much like death and taxes (I would rank it #2 here just behind taxes—that is, on a bad estimated-payments year). We know it isn't going to be the most pleasurable of experiences...but here's the deal—with all the modern technology we have, all the brilliant technology, could somebody *please* find a way to put a silencer on the dentist drill?

I would argue that what is most painful is not the actual pain—but the anticipation of the pain, and the sound of that drill!

You know, waiting for that moment, when they hit a nerve that sends a sharp pain starting in your mouth and ending somewhere near your shoelaces. The kind of all-body shivering experience that in this case, unfortunately, happens in the dentist chair and not in the bedroom.

Now understand, modern dentistry has come a long way. The dentist rarely ever hits that nerve anymore. They are much more user-friendly now, than say, the "Jack Nicholson of *The Shining*" dentist from days gone by.

But here is where the drill comes in. We hear the sound. The drilling...the drilling...the sound...the drilling...the sound, more drilling. (I am reaching my per word count/per topic limit here; otherwise I could go on about forty-six more pages, but you get the point.)

And when you hear this sound, your whole body is tensing up for the moment when the doc could hit "pay dirt." It is literally painful waiting and anticipating the off chance he hits that nerve.

However, if they could somehow find a way to silence the drill, and after all, how hard could that be? Then at least a portion of this anticipated pain would be alleviated.

Maybe they could have soothing music come out of the drill. Something from *Les Miserables* would be nice.

Just a thought, but I would be happy to help subsidize anyone willing to come up with this invention. In fact, if I can get my dentist to use it, I might donate the entire proceeds from this book! Better yet—you will likely need a lot more money than that...so just make it Bill O'Reilly's next book (which I think would somehow link his Abraham Lincoln book and his Jesus Christ book and come to the conclusion that if MSNBC had higher ratings back then than FOX TV, neither of these historical figures would have been elected or anointed!).

The Simplest—AND BEST— Parenting Advice Ever

Sometimes the beauty of an idea is in its simplicity. See if you're with me here.

The best parenting advice I have ever heard was from the stage production of the sixties rebellion musical *Hair*. Not exactly a theatrical production known for its philosophical brilliance, I know, but hang in there for a couple of paragraphs.

In the theater production of the musical, there is a line where the father is giving advice to his son. One of the things he tells him is, "Do whatever you want to do…be whatever you want to be—as long as you don't hurt anyone else."

At first glance, not exactly mind-numbing psycho-breakthrough parenting expertise. But let it sink in for a moment. Read it again and think about it. The beauty is in the simplicity…simple and yet so true.

Just think, if all human beings on this fine planet would follow that simple advice, what a better place it would be.

If all parents would let this be their guiding principle when raising their kids: "Do whatever you want to do. Be whatever you want to be. As long as you don't hurt anybody else."

Beautiful. Absolutely beautiful. All coming from a long-haired hippie father.

I heard this when I was about thirteen. And it has always stayed strong with me.

Political Smiles

Politics is like a baby...
an alimentary canal with a big appetite on one end, and absolutely no responsibility on the other.

Politics is the second oldest profession,
and it bears a striking resemblance to the first.

The word *politics*: derived from the word *poly*, meaning "many" and the word *ticks*, meaning "bloodsucking parasites."

When I was a boy, I was told anybody could become president.
I am beginning to believe it!
~Irving Stone
from his book *Clarence Darrow for the Defense*

Don't vote. You'll only encourage them.

Slogans that Make the Great State Irate

We love all fifty of our United States. Maybe some a little bit more than others. Here are some promotional slogans states have used—as seen on the website Top5.com.

ARKANSAS: The state of brotherly—and sisterly love!

ALABAMA: Keeping it in the family since 1819.

FLORIDA: More than just a great place to die.

IOWA: Our trees bend to the north because Minnesota sucks.

MISSISSIPPI: Keeping Louisiana from being dead last in just about every quality-of-life category.

MISSOURI: Missouri loves company.

MONTANA: Proud to welcome all anti-government-isolationist-compound conventions.

NEW JERSEY: What smell?

NEW YORK: Come for the skyline. Stay because you were mugged and don't have any money for the taxi to the airport.

NORTH DAKOTA: You don't want to visit here any more than we want to live here.

OKLAHOMA: Proudly named after an Indian tribe we slaughtered.

TEXAS: We kill 'em, so you don't have to!

WEST VIRGINIA: It seemed like a good idea at the time.

Does Geography Define Our Concern for Children?

I am always amazed at some of our staunch conservatives out there who live by the theme that we have to protect "America first."

They say something like, "We must take care of our own first," with proud patriotic bravado. Or they say, "Protect your own house first."

I say to that, "Really?" I understand the patriotism, and I, too, am proud of this great country. But isn't there a greater view?

It has always been curious to me why we care more for, say, the child in Utah, whom we do not know at all, than the child in India or Africa, whom we also do not know at all. Think about it. They both are babies or young children. Just because one is located in a geographical space somewhat closer to you, should that make you care about them more than others?

I would argue that it is a global world now. We need to expand our thinking. We are all part of the same team trying to stay alive and thrive here on beautiful Planet Earth. Let's do what's best for *all* kids— not just those kids here in America. To me, it is not that difficult of a concept.

Pride in our country is great. All peoples should be proud of where they live. But the bottom line is, both these kids are human beings. We know nothing about either one of them. Shouldn't we care for them both equally?

Just a thought…I will now hang up and listen for my answer (which should be interesting and probably for mature audiences only).

Eating for Epilepsy...Drinking for Dystrophy... Dancing for Dysentery...

...and any of the other multitude of occasions when we raise funds for a good cause by celebrating with a lavish fancy affair. Now, don't get me wrong. I fully appreciate the goodwill and good intentions of all the attendees at these fine events. And I certainly appreciate the funds donated to help so many organizations doing so much good for the underprivileged, sick, or any of the other many good causes out there.

But I have always felt a sort of weird uncomfortability, if not awkward uneasiness, at these affairs. Seeing people of affluence dressing up in full tuxedoed regalia, sipping on cocktails, eating appetizers, and experiencing fine dining followed by a big band–led night of dancing—all while supporting causes that range from people who may be homeless, starving, sick, abused, or in other completely desolate situations.

Am I the only one to catch the irony here?

Again, with the greatest of respect for the intentions of the "wine and dine and write a check" audience, I would submit that getting out in "the field" and directly working on projects might be a better way to spend your service time. I would argue that taking off the nice dress or the tuxedo, and instead directly involving yourself with the project or cause at hand would be much more rewarding, like helping to build a playground, organizing a project day at a needy school, working the front desk or the food line of a homeless shelter, visiting a kids' cancer hospital and talking to the kids, etc. You get the idea.

As fun as a night of dancing and liver pâté might be—I guarantee this direct contact with the folks in need of your services will 1) give you a much better intrinsic feeling when the project is complete, 2) help you better sell the cause to friends and family, 3) give you a much better understanding of what you are raising money for, and most important of all 4) encourage you to up the ante of your charitable giving by actually meeting the people you are helping firsthand...oh... and 5) give you less of a hangover the next day.

Now, please excuse me while I disembark and get off my high horse...but, hey, once in a while you have to saddle up and strap in for a bumpy ride.

Oh...and in the title to this topic, the first two events are real... the last one made up. Thankfully. Dancing for Dysentery is not an actual fund-raiser—at least I hope not—as it could make for a *really* long evening!

Sign of the Times

Here is an actual sign posted at a golf club in Scottsdale, Arizona:

Back straight, knees bent, feet shoulder-width apart.
Form a loose grip…not too tight.
Keep your head down the whole time.
Avoid a quick backswing.
Stay out of the water.
If you are taking too long, let others go ahead of you.
Try not to hit anyone.
Don't stand directly in front of others.
Quiet please, while others are getting ready to go.
Whatever you do, do not take any extra strokes!

GOOD. NOW REMEMBER TO FLUSH,
WASH YOUR HANDS,
AND GET READY FOR YOUR TEE TIME!

Exercise Our Way Out of Teen Troubles?

Let me ask you this: How many times have you seen a troubled kid, regardless of background or home situation, who runs or works out on a regular basis? I'm not talking about football or basketball practice; I am talking about a good, solid distance run in which they get the cardio going and really work up a sweat.

My guess is, not often. And herein lies a potential problem-buster.

Those endorphins that get released through exercise absolutely send something through your system that is all positive and feel-good. No matter how bad or lazy or down you feel before a good run, afterwards—always…I mean, always—without fail—you do feel better. About yourself. About others. About life.

It gives you kind of a cathartic blood rush that energizes your whole body. And I am by no means an avid runner. Just a recreational one. But I profess to the benefits of it, and especially how it could help some of our youth who occasionally struggle to stay on the straight and narrow.

Here is the point. You get some of these troubled teens doing some serious cardio work on a regular basis? Get them to exercise and push their physical limits? I would bet dimes to dollars that it would make a significant dent in the crime and discipline problems we have in school and on the streets.

How we do this? Different story, and not so easy. But in a later segment on the reorganization of the school day, I do offer a proposal.

Oh…and as some legitimate proof of what I profess here, I am pretty sure the success rates of the Teen Boot Camps that some courtroom judges have sent kids to—instead of jail—have been pretty successful. At these boot camps, kids are pushed to their physical limits—and when doing so, they often respond in a much more societally positive way.

Laugh Trax

There was the story of the guy who had a dog named "Twice."
When asked why he called him by that strange name,
he replied simply, "He never came when I called him once."

Sorry, Chicago fans, but we had to throw this one in:
You know why the Bears are so bad?
Because they started out as Cubs.

"One hundred fifty people were in the Kmart when they suddenly
announced a blue-light special in the ladies' lingerie section.
There were no survivors."
~Jimmy Fallon
The Tonight Show

"If I flunk a quiz on heredity,
can I blame it on my parents?"
~*Frazz* comic strip by Jeff Mallot

Someone once asked me, if I could interview anyone,
living or dead, who would it be?
I said, "The living one."

Note-a-Holics Anonymous?

This is not a serious topic…but I am looking for some help.

I know there are many support groups out there. But I don't think they have one for people like me, who have developed a serious note obsession. Again, we are not talking major disease control here, but my case has gone from worrisome, to bad, to much, much worse.

Doctors will not speculate…but my wife has estimated that if it continues or gets worse, my life expectancy could be three years. At best.

My defense: Understand first, my short-term memory is absolutely shot. Can't remember anything if it is not written down. Ideas will pop into my head, and one minute later, *boom!*—gone-zo—can't remember a thing. A brilliant idea (like writing a book!) is immediately forgotten and sadly irretrievable.

As a result, my go-to coping mechanism has become the notepad. Lots of them, sadly.

This is how bad it has gotten…I have four active notepads with me at all times. I've got my long-term to-do list, my short-term to-do list, my today to-do list, and my tomorrow to-do list. And that is just the start. These are on four separate small white notepads. Then, on a white eight-and-a-half-by-eleven-inch notepad, I keep another list, which has groceries to buy, movies to watch, restaurants I want to check out, friends to keep in touch with, etc.

This has become a sickness, no doubt. But I literally cannot function without my notepads.

Oh…I almost forgot about the notepad with the list of things that my wife needs to do, and a list for each of my two boys. It's the only way I can remember items needed to be done by them. It's just my way of giving them gentle, friendly, occasional reminders.

By the way, their response to this is neither gentle, nor friendly, and often is followed by the closest available object being thrown at a trajectory somewhere near my lower extremities.

Just asking…if anyone has any self-help ideas for this less-than-drastic affliction, please send me an email. ASAP…. Better yet, send money to help.

Or if you actually want me to read it, just send a note.

The clock is ticking here, folks.

Think Tank

There was the young man who consistently prayed to God for a bike.
But it never seemed to work.
So he stole a bike instead and then prayed for forgiveness.

Remember, if plan A does not work out,
there are twenty-five other letters to work with.

A nice old lady bought a new dog and sent it to obedience school.
After a week of school, she still could not get her dog to obey the
simple command to "sit."
She asked the trainer why the dog wouldn't sit and wouldn't obey.
The trainer said, "One of the things we are teaching him is
to question authority."

Live your life in *exclamation*,
not *explanation*.

Follow Your Dreams—
Except the one where you are at school wearing only underwear.

A Great Philosophy on Life—
Live one day at a time, and scratch where it itches.

Politicians, Are You Serious?

It is amazing to me, in this day and age, when negativity toward politics and politicians is so strong, that so few of our esteemed representatives have figured out that significant change is needed—that if they want to get elected, they need to break the mold. Check that. Not just break the mold, but shatter the mold. I am not even sure what the "mold" is, but if it is political campaigns as they are now—just blow that baby up big-time!

I mean, c'mon, folks…. It's obvious that people (the American public) are ready for something different in their politicians, and in particular their political campaigns. In tone, in style, in demeanor, in everything!

As I write this book, we are stuck in another election cycle of negative ads, millions in campaign donations, rhetorical speeches, debates where candidates rip on each other and avoid answering specific questions like it's the Black Plague.

Same old, same old, same old, same old.

No one, not one single candidate, has jumped on the "and now for something completely different" bandwagon?

And when I say completely different, I mean COMPLETELY different. Total landscape renovation.

Now, it is, of course, easy to complain, but much harder to provide a remedy. So, as a public service to both one and all—especially all—we provide our solutions right here in your user-friendly STUFF book. All for the cost of whatever you might have paid for this fine literary manual.

So, here they are. Three different things politicians should do to get elected in a heartbeat—or less.

1. Compliment your opponent—don't rip on him. Forget the ridiculous negative advertising. Put away the typical politically motivated insults. People are so burned out by this rhetoric! Shock the political world and actually say that your opponent is a decent guy, or a nice woman who has done good things, but… that you think you can do better. Respect the opponent, compliment the opponent, but also explain why you might be more effective. No more negative advertising! People are tired of it. Period. End quote.

2. Stop campaigning! That is right…stop campaigning (at least in the traditional way). Instead, continue to do the job you were elected to do and are currently working at. Do not spend much time campaigning at all. People are tired and burned out of the long, full-time dedicated campaign tours and campaign stops and media blitz, etc.

Saying something like this, I believe, would play incredibly well… "Folks, I was elected as the representative for the sixteenth district, and that is a full-time job. I plan to work full-time for the people who elected me and for the taxpayers who pay my salary. I will *not* spend the better part of the next year campaigning for my next job. However, I am going to run for senator of the state next year. I would love to represent you and the state as your proud senator. I will put out position statements that explain my views. I will debate at specific times with my opponent. I will meet with newspaper and media review boards so that I can accurately portray my philosophy and plan. But again, I will not spend the majority of my time campaigning because I was elected to be your state representative, and I will continue to put full-time efforts into that job."

Wouldn't that be refreshing to hear? Folks would just eat that up. Again, something completely different.

Finally…in my recipe for political success…

1. Say something to this effect: "I will not accept or request any campaign donations. My campaign will be my position statements, debates, etc. If this is not enough, so be it. But I will *not* take your valuable hard-earned money and spend it on the nausea of negative campaigning. Further…any of you out there who have extra money to spend—while any donation to my campaign is much appreciated—we would much rather have you give this money to a worthwhile needy organization. Thank you for your support."

Wow! Wouldn't that be a welcome change of pace! This would be a shocker, no doubt. But wouldn't this statement and this approach be a better alternative? Wouldn't people be drawn to this kind of thinking?

So there you have it. Three simple things. Total change from the current landscape. Rip up that old foundation. Shake that baby up from top to bottom. A refreshing change it would be!

To review: Less time spent on campaigning, zero money given to the political candidates, and actually complimenting and respecting your opponent. Completely different approach, no doubt, but I am fully confident it would work in today's political environment—if any would dare to try.

I have thought about running for office myself, but I quickly realized that there would be intensive background checks and personal scrutiny. I am not totally sure what I have done wrong or embarrassing in the past (a few things come to mind), but I am quite confident that with today's Internet-generated thoroughness, they would find enough to make me regret running. Maybe even enough to regret writing this book.

Can you call it fear of the unknown?

Jon Cohn

Up the Down Staircase

It doesn't matter if you are going up or going down. Stairs are always the better way to go!

I recently moved into a building with a nice park outside, just below the building (at least that is what the brochure said). There is an easily accessible set of stairs to get down to the park...but if you watch, almost everybody takes the elevator. Not the stairs. They do so, it seems, in almost a robotic, acceptance kind of way.

You know the routine—push button, open door, look away from stranger in elevator, door opens, walk out...*boom!* You, too, have arrived at your destination via transit express elevator—without hardly exerting any energy!

Why the elevator over the dreaded steps? Force of habit? An unwillingness to break from routine? It figures that way as people seem to naturally gravitate to the elevator without much thought process.

Well, folks, I would argue that if you don't want to gravitate somewhere else too soon (that place being below ground level and very sedentary), you might want to think about taking those steps.

Nothing like getting the heart pumping and the old cardiovascular system a little jump-start.

Here's the deal: If you live forty-four floors up, okay, you're off the hook. If it is ten degrees outside with a twenty-mile-per-hour wind—you get a mulligan.

But otherwise, do yourself a favor...take a hike—up the down staircase.

AUTHOR'S NOTE: In addition, you might be afflicted, as I have been of late, by the disease heretofore to be named FOECB. Very unscientifically meaning, Fear of Elevator Cable Breaking. I have only a mild condition now, but it is getting worse, and the prognosis: not good for the future.

Something about me being thirty stories up and my entire life's existence dependent on an unseen cable that is inspected once a year...and that is on a good year (usually an election year).

Thanks anyways, I'll take the stairs.

Miles of Smiles

The trouble with born-again Christians?
They're even a bigger pain the second time around.

A cruise ship is just a bad play surrounded by water.

"Everybody should believe in something...
I believe I'll have another drink."
~W. C. Fields

Second grader to his teacher:
"All right, all right. I will learn to read.
But once I do, I am never picking up another book again."

If you want to know who loves you more, your wife or your dog,
try this test:
Lock them both in the garage for a half hour.
Then open the door.
Now, see which one is happiest to see you.

The grandmother in the family was very health-conscious.
She walked five miles every day beginning at age sixty.
She's ninety-seven now, and they have no idea where the hell she is.

Bumper Sticker Snickers

As seen on the backs of cars across America…

HORN BROKEN. WATCH FOR FINGER INSTEAD.

I SAID NO TO DRUGS…BUT THEY JUST WOULDN'T LISTEN.

MY KID HAD SEX WITH YOUR HONOR ROLL STUDENT.

JESUS IS COMING…LOOK BUSY.

I HAVE GOOD BRAKES. DO YOU HAVE GOOD INSURANCE?

EVERYTHING I NEEDED TO LEARN I LEARNED IN PRISON.
HAVE A NICE DAY!

I WORK AT HOKEY POKEY CLINIC—
A GREAT PLACE TO TURN YOUR LIFE AROUND.

YOUR HONKING IS NOT GOING TO MAKE ME TEXT ANY FASTER.

Consultants?

Never have figured out exactly what the "consultant" does?

If I hear people have left a job and are now "consulting," I am automatically suspicious. Usually, out of work and consulting means: Got let go at work and now looking for an actual job.

"Oh yeah, I am doing some consulting work" is the modern-day equivalent of, "I smoked pot when I was younger but never inhaled."

Certainly, many consultants do quality and valuable work, of course. But do we depend on them too much?

Oh…and that goes double for municipalities, school districts, villages, and more that hire "consulting firms" and pay them thousands of dollars to give them an "overview" of their parks, or schools, or streets, etc.

Hogwash.

Instead of paying outside consultants, gather people who live in the town and use the town'facilities and let them be the "consultants." They're the ones who know the situation best. They're the ones most invested. Plenty of sharp minds with ideas and creative suggestions are almost always "in house."

So stop dishing out thousands of dollars to these high-paid consultant companies, and tap your best resource, whose services are free. The people who live and work there.

On Second Thought...

A guy is at the supermarket and notices a beautiful blond-haired girl waving at him. She comes over to say hello, and he is quite taken aback because he can't place where he knows her from.

So he says, "Do you know me?"

To which she replies, "I think you're the father of one of my kids."

Now his mind travels back to the only time he ever has been unfaithful to his wife, and he says, "My God, are you the stripper from my bachelor party that I laid on the pool table with all my buddies watching, while your partner whipped me with wet celery and then stuck a carrot up my butt?"

"No," she says as she looks him calmly in the eyes. "I'm your son's math teacher."

RAH RAH (Real American Heroes)
Part 1

have always had complete and unwavering respect for those who work on a daily basis with the sick and elderly in our society. These folks go about their job with not much fanfare and not many personal rewards, but the service they provide, of course, is oh, so valuable.

Recently, I saw a middle-aged man taking an elderly woman out of a passenger van and into a medical building. He was an employee of the senior center where she lived. He very gently took her arm and helped her balance. Talking to her, and smiling the whole time. Really trying to make the elderly lady feel comfortable.

Here is a guy who could just as easily be going through the motions of his job. He's probably not getting paid that much, but he takes what could be a tough and mundane job and brings it to the next level. With enthusiasm, he helps the frail lady out of the van and walks her all the way inside on a cold, wintry Chicago day. All while smiling and joking with her.

That is above and beyond the call of duty. Under the radar, largely out of the public view, and without much fanfare at all—just one of many fine people in this world doing a tough job without much pay—but doing it to the best of their ability and doing it with enthusiasm.

I give these folks a STUFF book RAH! RAH! because they are in my opinion Real American Heroes!

Poem

SLOW DANCE

Have you ever watched kids on a merry-go-round?
Or listened to the rain, slapping at the ground?
Ever follow a butterfly's erratic flight?
You better slow down.
Don't dance so fast.
Time is short.
The music won't last.
Did you run through each day
On the fly?
When you ask, "How are you?" do you hear the reply?
When the day is done, do you lie in your bed
With the next hundred chores, running through your head?
You better slow down,
Don't dance so fast.
Time is short.
The music won't last.
Ever told your child, we will do it tomorrow
And in your haste, not to see his sorrow?
Ever lost touch, and let a good friendship die?
'Cause you never had time, to call and say hi?
Don't dance so fast.
Time is short.

The music won't last.

When you run so fast to get somewhere, you miss half the fun of getting there.

When you worry and hurry through your day,

It's like an unopened gift…thrown away.

Life is not a race.

Do take it slower.

Hear the music,

Before the song is over.

> This poem is put out by the American Cancer Society. There is some question as to whether it was written by a young girl dying of cancer, or if it was written by a staff psychologist to help with ACS donations—if you can get past the controversy, *the message stands strong.*

The Two Most Important People

This next bit of incredibly insightful advice (cue laughter cards) is particularly geared for our "new to the workplace" young adults.

After having worked in a school, a recreation department, and a couple of miscellaneous office-type environments, I have become convinced that the key to success in all of these various workplaces is getting on the right side of two crucial people. Two that you might not otherwise think of right off the bat when thinking "key contacts." But these are people who can make life miserable for you or silky smooth, depending on how well you get to know them and how you treat them.

Note that this advice holds true regardless of the work environment.

Surprisingly, I have found that it is not the boss, not the vice president, not the head of sales, not even the head of personnel whom you really need to get in good with. No, the key to success and to a reasonably enjoyable work experience is getting on the good side of 1) the front desk receptionist, and 2) the custodian.

That's right, gang. If you develop a good relationship with these two, your work life will get off to a great start. The rest is a piece of cake.

These two underrated, but critically important people can make your life immeasurably easier in so many ways. Or they can grind you down like fine limestone under a construction drill.

Remember, bosses come and go. Top-level execs come and go. Vice presidents and middle management personnel not only come and go—they have more movement than an Ex-Lax convention. And marketing and salespeople? Those folks will jump at the chance to go. Any chance.

But receptionists and custodians? They are there for the long haul. And not just there, but they are the "rocks," the foundation and stability upon which the office operates. They can help in so many ways.

If it is keys you need, or something to be fixed, or information about a client, or maybe even inside knowledge about a coworker you think might be cheating on either his budget report or his wife (or both!), it is the friendly face at the front desk or the one with the tool belt who can help the most.

If you're dealing with a coworker, an angry parent, an emergency at home, or if your car breaks down in the parking lot, these two bastions of the lower rung of the office economics scale are the ones who will come to your rescue.

Trust me on this. Treat these people well, folks. Treat them with the respect they deserve. The rewards are plentiful. The regrets—may be even worse.

The Pledge of the Planet Earth

Here's the idea. It is based on our country and our use of the "Pledge of Allegiance."

Clearly the Pledge of Allegiance is a very nice tradition that we have here in this country, and one that I think is very positive. I choose at this time not to get into the controversy about the "one nation under God" wording except to say to those, like myself, who don't necessarily "believe"—relax, take a deep breath, and maybe don't take things quite so seriously. (A hint about how even a non-traditional religionist like myself views the use of the word "God" in the Pledge of Allegiance.)

But the point here is…why not come up with a "Pledge" that includes the entire planet—all countries and all people?

Why not have a pledge that all kids throughout the world could recite at the start of their school day and for special functions? This pledge would go beyond each country's own anthem or pledge, and instead include all civilizations and all peoples living here on earth.

A little global "Kumbaya" never hurt anyone.

What a wonderful message to get to kids at an early age, that yes, country allegiance is important. But first and most important is for all of us—different countries, different cultures, to get along and work together for the greater good.

So here is my idea. It is called the "Pledge of the Planet"—to be recited by all school kids at start of each day. In all schools throughout the world.

It would go something like this:

> "I pledge to this Planet Earth, and all the people who inhabit it,
>
> My full love, support, and respect.

To be kind and considerate of all others who live here.

And to help out our fellow humankind in any way we can.

And to remember that we are all one.

To respect each other; to celebrate our differences; and to always help those most in need.

Our goal together: Peace, freedom, happiness, and health to all.

Together we can. Together we are one."

Not Easy Getting Old

Three golfers are walking down the fairway.

"Sixty is the worst age to be," said the sixty-year-old. "You always feel like you have to pee. And most of the time nothing happens."

"Ah, that's nothing," said the seventy-year-old. "When you're seventy, you don't have a bowel movement anymore. You take laxatives, eat bran, you sit on the toilet all day, and nothing happens."

"Actually," said the eighty-year-old, "eighty is the worst age of all."

"Do you have trouble peeing, too?" asked the sixty-year-old.

"No, I pee every morning at six a.m. I pee like a racehorse; no problem at all."

"Do you have trouble having a bowel movement?" asked the seventy-year-old.

"No, I have one every morning at six thirty a.m."

Puzzled with this, the sixty-year-old said, "Let's get this straight. You pee every morning at six a.m. and poop every morning at six thirty a.m. So what's so tough about being eighty?"

"I don't wake up until seven."

(Source: Aha-Jokes.com)

Jon Cohn

Slice of America—As Good As It Gets

Here is my vote for the best representation of pure good times—which are legal and moral that our fine country has to offer.

Many possibilities here, of course. But I would like to nominate the college football tailgate party. What a great tradition, and what a perfect example of everyone just plain having a great time!

There have been times, and I know I am probably a party of one here, when I have gone to a game with no interest in going to see the actual game. Many times I don't even know anyone who is going to be there!

But I will just walk around the stadium and/or the collegiate institution and watch the tailgaters. I soak up the smells, the smiles, the atmosphere, and the prevailing "feel good" atmosphere that a tailgate has to offer.

Thank goodness there are no citations given out for "tailgate stalker," because I would be guilty as charged!

I find the fresh air, the enthusiasm, and the big game atmosphere almost Zen-like therapy for me.

I may then go home to watch the game on TV (tape delay, of course) after having enjoyed the awesome pregame atmosphere.

What is so great about the "tailgate party"? Why is it the perfect example of Americans having a good time?

Hard to explain, but let's try this:

Let's mix the ingredients here. First, you have America's game—football—then you throw in everyone's favorite pastime—eating! Add a little of the classic autumn cool but sunny weather so many of us enjoy…bring in some good friends…and best of all, everyone seems to be in a great mood. It is just an uplifting atmosphere. Hard to find any spoiler alerts at college football tailgating.

Oh…and don't forget the cardiovascular exercise free game of bags that is so popular now at tailgating parties. As a complete side note, after developing the Midwestern Soft Twist Pullback technique (next book, not now), I have been nearly unbeatable in this game.

So, I nominate the college football tailgate party as the best example of good old, unadulterated, pure fun and enjoyment that our country has to offer. Feel free to let me know your nominations at jcsportsandtees@aol.com—but I warn you in advance—any votes for the company picnic, or a trip to any mega-amusement park, or anything on late-night adult television will be deleted immediately.

Jon Cohn

No Respect

Some great Rodney Dangerfield lines here:

"I get no respect, no respect at all."

"It's been a rough day. I got up this morning…
put a shirt on and the button fell off.
I picked up my briefcase, and the handle came off.
Now I'm afraid to go to the bathroom!"

"My dog was really something.
We used to call him Egypt because he left a pyramid in every room."

"I was so poor growing up, if I wasn't born a boy,
I would have had nothing to play with."

"I was so ugly as a baby, my mother had morning sickness
after I was born."

"I remember when I swallowed a bottle of sleeping pills.
I called my doctor. He told me to have a few drinks
and get some rest."

"My sister had such a bad reputation in high school. I mean it was so bad her yearbook picture was horizontal."

"The hotel I just stayed at was really cheap. I mean, really cheap. They were so cheap, they stole my towels!"

To Be (Vegan) or Not to Be

I have always been the standard meat-eating American food consumer. No problem. Not much thought to it, really. Until lately.

Due to a mid-forties battle with high cholesterol, I've mostly stayed away from red meat, with the occasional steak or hamburger still being consumed with equal parts deranged enjoyment and spineless guilt.

And don't even get me started with the barbecued pulled pork sandwich—one of my great weaknesses, and one with which I have had a long-standing one-way romance. I cannot tell you how depressed I was when my doctor told me that pork really isn't the "other white meat" when it comes to affecting cholesterol level. (Damn!)

But recently, I had some discussions with people who are vegans. Yes, vegans are people, too. And although I have not yet entered the secret and sordid world of the Veganese, I have at least ordered their tourism brochure and am starting to read through it, shall we say.

Basically, as I understand it (I am sure vegan vets will tell me I don't), vegans stay away from any products that come from animals— primarily because of the mistreatment of animals in the development and creation of the food.

The mistreatment doesn't just include killing them. No, I am finding out it is far worse than that, such as caging them in areas so tight they can barely move, feeding them so much they almost explode, chopping off certain body parts before actually killing the whole animal, and a variety of other depressing-to-find-out techniques.

This is one of these…the-less-you-know-the-better scenarios.

But we *should* know. And we do know—if we take the little bit of time to find out. And the problem is, once you start hearing about this mistreatment, or worse yet, if you have seen pictures (the visuals stay with you), and it can definitely have an effect.

Bottom line is, if you really think about what those precious animals have to go through (note the use of the word *precious* to increase reader guilt factor), it can, indeed, give you pause about what you are about to eat.

Fair warning. I am not there yet. But vegans out there, I am starting to see the light. I am starting to lean to the V, shall we say! I may soon cross over and hope I will be accepted with open arms—if not closed lips. You may have a new team member in the not-too-distant future.

My only concern, though, is that the steady diet of roughage, tofu, and pine nuts, while delicious, may cause a little bit of traffic backup in the digestive system when eaten exclusively, if you know what I don't really mean.

Next topic. Please!

My Vote: Two Best Comedic Lines of All Time

Let's talk comedy here for just a minute. I have always loved humor and comedy. The old expression "laughter is the best medicine" is one I have always believed in.

Here are my votes, in the comedy categories of 1) Guys who absolutely crack me up, 2) Funniest lines of all time, and 3) Best comedian of all time.

(Send me your votes at jcsportsandtees@aol.com, and I will post them on our STUFF People Might Want to Know website.)

Now, no doubt I have laughed many times in my five-plus decades, but rarely have I been doubled over, cramping from laughing so hard and nearly brought to absolute tears. The two guys who can do that to me are the late, great Rodney Dangerfield and Don Rickles. Both comic icons, of course. When those guys get on a roll (Rodney with the "no respect" and Rickles with the insults), they fire out jokes like bullets out of an AK-47. One right after another, building on each other. Momentum picking up as they go. And the audience, of course, is fair game.

Everyone has their own funny bone—for me, it was these two guys. When they got on a roll, they not only tickled my funny bone, they split that baby right in two.

Next: Funniest lines of all time—my vote: A tie.

1. Groucho Marx
    "I refuse to join this club! I would never join any club that would have me as a member!"

2. Rodney Dangerfield

"I get no respect, no respect at all. Even my mother never loved me. That's right, I tell ya, she never loved me. I mean, she breast-fed my brother and said she liked me as a friend."

Finally my vote for: Best comedian of all time

In a tremendous battle among worthy compatriots...I am going with an upset special!

Curly of the Three Stooges.

This guy was the best! Similar to the great athletes who do things you just can't teach, Curly in those *Three Stooges* clips did things you absolutely cannot script. Wacky, bizarre, but most of all silly, with some classic lines to offset his physical humor, Curly was the Michelangelo of crazy comedy. And *The Three Stooges*? As good to me today as a near senior citizen as they were when I was a seven-year-old kid watching them pound the heck out of each other.

The fact that I have passed on this love of the Stooges to my two now young adult sons (both are big fans), I consider one of the great accomplishments of my parenting career. The tradition lives on! (To put it mildly, Mom did not exactly relish this particular tradition... might be an X-chromosome, Y-chromosome thing.)

Not New, but True

You have heard this before, but it is so strong. So good. So simple. So dead-on accurate that it bears repeating. In fact, better than repeating, it bears using.

Here is the simple truth given by some old sage from days gone by…

The saying goes something like this: "You can judge the character of a person by how they treat service people."

B32… O74… N42… Bingo! So true. Thank you, old sage, wherever you are.

Just watch how someone interacts with the restaurant waiter, the hotel front desk person, the taxi cab driver, the ticket-taker at the airport, the barber, the hairdresser…you get the idea.

Observe the interaction. You will see a variety of attitudes in these situations, and they are all so telling. Maybe calling them a window into the soul of a person is going a bit overboard, but don't underestimate the power of simple. And here, the attitude tells an awful lot about the person.

Your user-friendly STUFF book breaks it down for you very non-scientifically. See if you can recognize any of the three primary categories people fall into here:

We describe them anatomically and homogenously (not sure what that really means, but it does sound awfully scholarly—so let's go with it).

1. The "see me, serve me" Homo sapien. This is the fine individual who either vociferously or much more subtly makes sure the person working knows they are in a position of serving. Demanding little things to be done, making changes without any appreciation

of the difficulty it could be causing, finding items to make the service person go on the defensive, and generally, and again it is often subtle, putting themselves in a position of superiority over the service person who is working.

2. The "I can't see you, you aren't important to me" Homo platypus. This is the person who tends to ignore the service person. Rarely making eye contact. Going about their business oblivious to the work and effort of the service provider. The "I can't see you" species are not as annoying as the demanding "see me, serve me," crustacean, but still they roam somewhere below sea level, in the ocean, that is their basic treatment of other human beings.

3. The "respect the worker" Homo humane-a-scopic person. This is the individual who actually takes notice of the service person's work and effort. They step outside their own world and appreciate that the worker is probably working long hours and not at the most glamorous of jobs. Simple thank-yous for filling up the water, leading you to your seat, clearing the table, or maybe changing a ticket, all done with a bit of actual eye contact, and sincere appreciation can truly go a long way.

Again, we are not talking Einsteinian rocket scientry here. Really, just a simple observation of people and how they deal with others.

But if you are a boss hiring an individual, or you are choosing between new friends you have just met, or for our readers out there in the vast and frighteningly unforeseen world of the dreaded dating scene—these simple behaviors and simple attitude indicators can tell you oh, so very much about the character and kindness of the person you are trying to get to know.

Critical info, no doubt. And the beauty is in the simplicity. Just watch and observe.

You think about these three different types of people. And you think of how this small but telling personality trait could carry over into long-term job performance, or personnel relationships. Think real hard. And then you can better decide whom you want to invest your time with.

Just some friendly advice from a struggling first-time writer.

First Installment—MBHS

I am a longtime collector of quotes and sayings. Some famous. Some not so well-known, but still meaningful to me.

Hopefully you have some of your own that inspire you.

One that I recently heard that has become part of my core group philosophies for life is by Maya Angelou, the famous poet, educator, teacher, and philosopher who passed away in early 2014. I really didn't know much about her, sadly, until she passed away—but then after reading about her, I realized what an amazing person she truly was.

The one quote that stuck with me was when she said, "I tried to put a silver lining in someone's cloud every day."

What a sweet and simple but powerful thought. Really solid. We all have great aspirations and great goals, and it is wonderful that we work to achieve them. But along with those lofty goals we should remember that just to do something nice every day, something to lift up the spirits of someone every single day—is meaningful, as well.

That's a great goal to shoot for. And one that's easy to achieve.

This is where the MBHS comes in. We all hear great quotes—inspirational ones that particularly move us. Maybe we remember them for a day or two. But too often over time that quote that so much hit home with you gets forgotten. The thought behind it fades.

This is a shame, as some of those great thoughts or quotes can help guide you to maybe living your life just a little bit better.

What we need to do is to get those quotes and philosophies front and center in our mind on a regular basis—a constant reminder, so that they don't fade way, and so that they can help you to improve at least some part of your life.

So this is why I have coined the phrase MBHS, which stands for Mind, Body, Heart, Soul.

In order for these inspirational thoughts to stay with us and actually make a difference, you have to adopt them strongly...in other words, bring it into your MBHS.

Whether it means writing them down somewhere, starting each day with the reminder, keeping a list in your office—whatever technique you use, don't let the thought fade.

Keep it strong. Keep it in your MBHS. And collectively, it can help make you more the person you want to truly be.

More quotes and sayings to come in this book, but Maya Angelou and her simple and easily attainable "Put a silver lining in someone's cloud every day" really stuck with me. And I do try to put it in action every single day.

The "Morning Break" Radio Show

I did a radio show a while back called the *Morning Break*. To put it kindly, it was not exactly on a major station in Chicago. We were on right after the Russian morning talk show called *Echo of the Planet* (don't ask), and we preceded, I believe, a show featuring the best in Hungarian music.

Not exactly a recipe for supplanting Howard Stern. Our motto was "best show on radio—all we need is listeners!"

We battled long and hard against all odds, and we had a great time doing it. What a cast of characters we had. Our producer was Kevin "The Swamp Ratt" Horan. We had help behind the scenes from Josh "The Waterboy" Fox, "Bigg John" Polladian, and Mike "The Iceman" Laurie. Our production department had some big boys working in it and it looked at times like an NFL offensive line. But as big as they were, their hearts and their helpfulness were just as great.

Behind the scenes and generally managing were assistant station manager Jorge "*No Pantelones*" Murillo, and the station manager Mark "The Czar" Pinski. Not to mention for an all too brief time, the semi-brilliance of Danny "Rock Chalk" Zederman.

On air besides myself ("the Coach"), there were Brian "The Boy Toy" Bauer, Joel "Bigg Dogg" Radwanski, Mark Carmen (somehow escaped a nickname), Frankie "Beans" Barber, Matt "Kid K" Kolsky, Brady Stiff (didn't need a nickname—too easy), and Neal "No Stones" Malones, among many others.

It was a heck of a crew, and even though we made fun of the obscurity of our show and our ratings…behind the humor and self-deprecation, we all thought we put together a damn good show.

It was sports talk–based, but we got off-topic early and often and always used humor to keep ourselves, and callers, from getting too serious.

We couldn't get any major station to pick us up, and after a while we had to give up the dream. But I remain convinced, still today, that we could have made it big if given the opportunity and a little bit of coaching.

We found out quickly that the radio world is quite in-bred. Personalities switch from station to station, as do the program directors and the general managers. Through it all, they seem to keep hiring the same people—just for different slots. We found it, unfortunately, a tough nut to crack.

The takeaway from this experience is 1) never regret doing something you love to do, and 2) for people hiring and looking to fill open job opportunities, don't get too comfortable with people you are familiar with—never be afraid to look outside the box and try new people and new things. No risk, no reward!

But again, the *Morning Break* radio show involved a lot of great people having some fun and trying to put out an entertaining product. I will always remember those days fondly.

Nobody Asked, But

And remember, the second choice title for this book was *In No Particular Order*. So, we take yet another random curve and slide over into…

My rankings of the three best smells known to humankind.

Or we can upgrade this section and call it olfactory pleasantries, for those who want to make this sound more official than it actually is.

Here is this much-anticipated list:

1. The aroma of brand-new coffee when you take the aluminum wrap sealing off the new carton. Immediately after opening, stick your nose right near the lid or rim to get the full rich aroma. Excellent! The richness and smell of the coffee, right on release, just permeates beautifully as it spreads to all corners of the kitchen.

2. The smell of burning leaves in the autumn (unfortunately, illegal now, but when someone does it anyway, and you are outdoors in a yard nearby…oh man, is that smell good!). The autumnal crisp air adds as a flavor-enhancer, but the burning leaves and their smell? Those old enough to remember the "good old days" know what I'm talking about.

3. The smell when you pass by a Garrett Popcorn Shop. They may be just a Chicago franchise, I am not sure. But whatever they've got going on inside to produce that smell to those of us outside? Well, whatever it is, it should be illegal in fifteen states. Bottom line, almost impossible to pass by without a quick stop in.

Laugh Trax

Before you criticize someone, you should walk a mile in their shoes.
That way, when you do criticize them, you're a mile away and you
have their shoes!

Sign seen on building door:
"Procrastination Convention.
Begins day after tomorrow."

What has four legs and an arm?
Answer: A very happy pit bull.

Guy asks the dentist, "My teeth are getting more yellow all the time.
What should I do?"
Dentist says, "Wear more brown ties."

Then there is the story about the guy who is a vegetarian—
not because he loves animals, but because he hates plants!

Guy goes into auto shop for work to repair brakes.
Comes to pick up the car, and the mechanic says,
"We couldn't fix the brakes, but we did adjust your horn
so it will blow much louder."

Too Pooped to Pope?

The new pope? Pope Francis? All I can say is…rock star! Absolutely love this guy as he does his little shake-me-up/shimmy-bop to the Catholic Church and its long-standing practices.

As a primarily non-religious facsimile of the human species myself (see later note on MOPED religion), I have become fascinated, if not excited about the recently named pope.

This guy is the goods.

A more understanding nature toward social issues and mores—long needed (to say the least) in the Catholic religion, and an emphasis on helping those most in need, have been a pleasure to see take place. Most importantly, he has not been afraid to shake up some papal feathers and ruffle a few robes.

It will be fun to watch as the pope hopefully has a long and productive stay in his lifetime-appointed position.

My only hope is that as this wunderkind of traditional religious upheaval gets older, he does not get too tired. Too worn out from dealing with all the traditionalists who certainly will give him resistance.

In short, I hope that as he ages into the future, he does not get… "Too pooped to pope!"

The Missing Link in First-Aid Training

Through my many years of coaching and being involved in sports, I have attended quite a few first-aid training seminars. The Red Cross test dummy and I have gotten well acquainted over the years. Although I do think it is more of a one-way appreciation in our relationship.

Anyhow…

Most of the first-aid seminars I've attended have been very helpful. Good injury prevention and emergency care knowledge is given out, and it's usually very helpful. Very often you get to practice hands-on training, and the materials provided are quite helpful. In addition, the instructors, for the most part, are well informed and enthusiastic in their desire to teach you. Typically you leave the training with a good understanding of emergency first-aid items (i.e., CPR), and you often have to pass a test to show your understanding.

So all in all…all is good.

But here is the one chink in the armor of first-aid training.

If you don't review the procedures constantly…if you leave the training and then go on with your daily activities over the next ten, to twenty, to thirty days, or the next couple of months, which turns into a couple of years, etc., you will begin to forget some of the items you learned…. If an emergency were to happen—and remember, it usually is a sudden panic situation—you might not have the immediate recall you need (even though you are first-aid-certified) to administer the emergency first aid.

Here is the missing link in the first-aid training. Not enough of these seminars emphasize the importance of review. They may mention it, but they don't emphasize it, and more importantly, they don't give you helpful advice on how to make reviewing a regular habit (after all, this could, at any point, save someone's life).

But here is where your friendly STUFF author comes to the rescue! (Assisted, of course, by my love-torn training dummy.)

I call it the smoke alarm copy. That's right, make it just like checking your smoke alarm batteries.

At the end of each month, take out your basic materials and review what you would do in certain first aid–related emergencies. Change the batteries, and think about what to do in a medical emergency. Turn the page of the calendar. Review your CPR. It only takes five minutes. Once you get in the habit, it becomes easy to remember.

Better yet, and this is a common coaching technique for a variety of sports—encourage mental repetitions. Go through in your mind different situations where an emergency may occur. Picture yourself coming across an individual who suddenly goes down with an apparent heart attack. What procedures would you do? Imagine a person having an epileptic attack at an event you are attending. What would you do? What is proper procedure?

Actually visualize yourself going through the check, call, and care procedures. This can be done any time. While you are driving. Sitting at home. Working out on the treadmill, or lying in bed before you go to sleep.

You never know when one of these medical emergencies can pop up. Usually when you least expect it.

If you have mentally prepared on a regular basis, in addition to the formal training, there is a much better chance that you won't panic when it happens and that you will keep calm and make the right decisions in what could sometimes be life-threatening situations.

This is one of these STUFF items that I hope you never have to use. But if you do…

Remember, as one wise first-aid test dummy once said (I think it was after a particularly bad mouth-to-mouth session), "If you fail to prepare, then you prepare to fail."

Simply Amazing

Imagine taking a cruise ride on the train of life. The one most of us take makes regular stops at what I call "Routine Station."

We get on, we get off, we get on, and we get off. Rinse, repeat, rinse, and repeat again. Routine station is a comfortable stop, no doubt. We know the people; we know places to go. We know the best places to eat.

But occasionally, we need to pass by that stop. As tempting as it is, ignore that opening door, hang on, and stick around for a few more stops.

My favorite stop? "The stop, watch, observe, and appreciate" station. Which comes directly before the "If you think about it, you could really be amazed" stop.

Both of these get-off points are way too often skipped by the "too busy getting through the daily necessities of life" passenger.

But—and here is the key—there are so many things around us that are simply amazing, that is, if you take a moment to think about them. Things that can give you internal joy and comfort, if you just let them. Take pause. Observe. Breathe deep. And see all the things that can amaze simply.

For example…see our next segment

MBHS Again!
Mind, Body, Heart, and Soul

Continuing in that vein, amazing things are everywhere if we take the time to stop and observe. They are above us, below us, beside us, and yes—even inside us, in our daily life.

Life is too short, folks. Now, I know everyone has heard that a million times! Most ponder the thought for a few seconds, maybe a minute for the really meditational, and then they move on to the next item. But that thought is a mind-set too valuable to let go so easily.

Which once again brings us to MBHS (Mind, Body, Heart, and Soul), MBHS being just a symbol for fully committing to something.

You could read this now and move on…or you could write it down, bookmark it, and tape it up somewhere. Any kind of finite reminder to make slowing down and noticing the beauty and wonder around you part of your daily routine and lifestyle.

Look around. Listen. Smell. Use all of your senses. And find ways in this life to be simply amazed. The beauty of it is, it doesn't cost a thing!

And it doesn't always have to be found in nature. It can be any items that you come across in your daily life.

I give you three examples, for me, of things that we may take for granted, but if we stop to think about them, they could surely—amaze simply.

Among those would be:

1. The fact that every morning at 6:20 a.m. I get a full-fledged, full-bodied, top-of-the-line newspaper delivered on my driveway—or being kind, at least somewhere in the nearby vicinity. This paper

includes stories and news items that happened the night before at 7:00, 8:00, sometimes as late as 11:00 p.m.—and here I am reading about it at 6:30 the next morning. Pretty amazing when you think about it. The covering of a story, the reporting, the printing, the editing, the writing, the layout, the design, and then—someone getting it out to the various locations for delivery, and *boom!* Six twenty a.m. sharp…paper delivered. Not just what happened the night before, but analysis and interviews included. Pretty amazing, if you stop and think about it.

2. The fact that I can hear a voice over the phone, an actual live sound from someone who may be talking in say, California. The person is three thousand miles away, and somehow I can hear their voice. I can hear the sound they are making from three thousand miles away. All carried across phone lines. It now is something we expect, even get mad about when it doesn't work. But if you stop and think about it…that sound somehow traveling all that distance? Pretty amazing.

3. And how about the human heart? Now, this one I don't like to think about too much, because, you know, I don't want to test fate, shall we say… but have you seen the pictures of the heart? More specifically, a film or video of it beating inside the human body? This is one complicated contraption! I mean, there is all kinds of stuff going on with each and every beat. We're talking aortic valves, ventricles, blood pumping, contractions, etc. The

thing works pretty hard, and a lot of pieces have to fall into place to make it all go smoothly. And for most of us, it does. For a long, long time. Beat after beat. No real breakdowns. I look at the incredibly complex makeup of this all-important organ, and then remember how it basically is the only thing keeping me alive. Again, don't think about this too much. Maybe out of sight, out of mind is the best philosophy here, but once again, pretty amazing if you stop to think about it, or better yet look at the picture or videos and see how it actually works. Simply amazing!

Speaking of the Morning Newspaper...

always tell people I can handle all of life's problems—all the troubles that may be thrown at me—as long as I have a cup of coffee and forty-five minutes with my morning newspaper first thing to start the day. If the day starts off with coffee and the quiet soaking up of the newspaper—then bring it on for the rest of the day! World hunger? Education reform? Climate change issues? Cubs' hundred-year drought in the World Series? *No problemo.* As long as I have had thirty minutes of quality time with my newspaper and coffee, I am good to go. Bring it on!

But start me out without my coffee and quiet reading time? Without that thirty-minute "transition" time? Getting the garage door open with the remote control might be too taxing for me. And my mood for the rest of the day? Somewhere between bad and brutal with a stop at ornery along the way.

And While We're on Coffee...

What is it with the people who drown their coffee in sugar and then drench it in cream?

Sorry, folks, that is gross! Nutritionally if not morally unacceptable, says Dr. Stuff.

I mean, a dash of sugar and/or a dash of cream in the coffee—you're all good. But all you out there who pour the coffee, but then load it up with equal parts sugar and cream…. No! No! No! And more *no!* Not good!

There is nothing like a good strong cup of straight black coffee first thing in the morning.

But if you must mix in the cream or sugar…moderation, my friends. Moderation.

Chuckle Break

After an afternoon of golf, several men were hanging out in the locker room socializing. A cell phone sitting on a bench began to ring. "I've got you on speakerphone," a man said after he answered the call.

"Hi, dear," came the voice on the other end. "I'm at the mall, and that beautiful diamond tennis bracelet I have been waiting for is on sale for three thousand dollars. Can I buy it?"

"Sure," the man said. "Is that it?"

"Not quite," the women replied. "On my way to the mall, I passed by the Jaguar dealership. They offered me a deal on a pre-owned vehicle for eighty thousand dollars, but I told them I'd have to speak with you first."

"Sounds like a steal," the man said. "Go for it."

"Really?"

"Sure, why not," the man replied.

"Well, there's just one more thing," the woman said. "There is a beautiful gown at my favorite boutique. They'll let me have it today for five thousand dollars."

"Whatever makes you happy," said the man.

"You're the best, honey," replied the woman. "I love you."

The man ended the call and set the cell phone down back on the bench, and then said out loud, "Hey, does anybody know whose phone this is?"

Think Tank

Too many people quit looking for work—once they find a job.

"The trouble with putting armor on is that
while it protects you from the pain,
it also protects you from the pleasure."
~Celeste Holm

The best exercise for your heart is picking up
the spirits of someone else.

The best way to gain self-respect?
Well, to start, stop worrying so much about self.

"You don't lose to cancer.
You beat cancer by how you live, why you live,
and the manner upon which you live."
~Stuart Scott
ESPN

We may not have arrived in the same ship,
but we're all in the same boat now.

Integrity

"Integrity is how you act when no one is watching. When no one knows what you're doing. It is always telling the truth, clearing up any misconceptions or partial truths. It is never knowingly hurting anybody or anything. Integrity is keeping our commitments."
~Steven W. Vannoy

"As we express our gratitude *we must never forget* that the highest appreciation is not to utter words, but to live by them."
~John F. Kennedy

Remember, the dogs may bark, but the caravan rolls on.

If you are busy rowing the boat, you don't have time to rock it.

When you point a finger at somebody, three of them are pointing right back at yourself.

"Nobody is better than you...and you are better than nobody."
~Joe Biden
(Describing his mom's lesson about humility and entitlement)

"What we have learned from history is that we really haven't learned from history."
~Mark Twain

Canning at the Intersection

Kudos to all you volunteers who give of your time to collect money for worthy causes out on the dangerous intersections of our busy four-way streets.

Your effort and commitment to a cause is noble indeed. And the fact you are risking both life and limb dodging in and out of cars only adds to this nobility.

I do, however, have only one request. Have a sign that tells me what you're collecting for. A big sign! One that most of us can easily and quickly read.

Because most of the time when people are walking up to my car, I have no idea what they're collecting for. This creates an unnecessary level of uncomfortability.

Maybe you are wearing a small sign or a T-shirt that's readable only as you get close. And you probably are wearing one of those neon-bright vests to help you be seen—but by the time you reach my car, you have already entered my personal space and now I am uncomfortable with your approach.

Additionally, once you get to my car (usually just a few seconds before the light is to turn green), there really isn't time for you to explain what you're doing.

So, please, we do want to help. I don't mind contributing to worthy organizations. And again, your dedication to be out there collecting for the cause is wonderful. And for that matter, my desire to rid myself of loose change is equally motivational.

But, please, let us know what it is you are collecting for—well in advance of approaching our car. A big sign would do the trick. Not just a yellow highlighter-type safety vest. But some kind of sign or information that immediately tells the motorist what the collection is for.

Oh...and if you could give out Ghirardelli chocolates instead of those "stick to the wrappers" lollipops...that would be appreciated, too!

Chuckle Time

"The trouble with being punctual
is that usually there is no one there to appreciate it."
~Harold Rome

"Hey, does the name Pavlov ring a bell?"

IRS Motto #1:
Be audit you can be.

IRS Motto #2:
We've got what it takes, to take what you've got.

Husband asks for breakfast in bed.
Wife says, "No problem. Just sleep in the kitchen."

I always said I wanted to become somebody.
I guess I should have been more specific.

Email passwords now must contain a capital, a letter, a number, a
plot, a protagonist with character development,
and a surprise ending.

RAH RAH (Real American Heroes)
Part 2

Another RAH RAH (Real American Hero) story.

This time we introduce you to a young man named Michael Trout. Actually, not so young anymore—sorry, Mike—but he was when he started his very unique mission.

Regular guy. Grew up in the Chicago suburbs. Went to Wheaton College, a devout and strict Christian school that demands old-school values and old-school tradition. They were most famous for the on-campus rule that did not allow students to hold hands in public. Really.

Now the college has loosened up a bit, and you can hold hands, but no kissing! Enrollment is not high (are you surprised?). But it has been a longtime fixture and a solid academic institution in the Chicago area for many years.

Mike, a feisty and passionate leader, was not so keen on all those rules, and he married his college love the day after graduation! Patience was not at the top of the list of adjectives to describe this young man.

So what did the couple do to make their impact on the world right out of college?

Like any normal college student right out of school, he moved to North Lawndale, one of the most dangerous and economically deprived neighborhoods in Chicago, and became a "minister" out on the streets. At night.

This involved hanging out on street corners and developing relationships with gangbangers, drug dealers, prostitutes, and many others. And did we mention he did this in the middle of the night? And did we mention that Mike was very "Anglo" and working in a largely African American neighborhood?

That's right, a twenty-one-year-old white kid being a night minister on the corner of Chicago's most dangerous neighborhood.

Sure beats being an intern at Merrill Lynch.

He got some much-needed assistance from a local African American minister, John Spikner, who took the young twenty-one-year-old under his wing and helped him gain entry to the neighborhood.

Mike would talk to the young men and consult with them. He listened to their problems and their often very difficult situations. He would offer advice, assistance, food, and money, whatever it took.

But most of all, he cared. And they could tell. He was able to make unique connections, with again, some of Chicago's toughest population.

He had a unique style that connected with many of the mostly young people he met.

Now here is the beautiful part of the story. This was not just a short-term, "do good" mission by a motivated, idealistic college kid (not that there is anything wrong with that at all).

But twenty years later, Mike is still at it!

His off-the-cuff, unsolicited street-corner ministering turned into a lifelong mission.

He formed an organization called YMEN (Young Men's Education Network), which, over the years, has helped many African American youth in the North Lawndale area. Over ninety of the young men have gone on to college, the military, and other meaningful careers.

He is strict with the young men. To belong, the kids must follow the rules. Yet Mike's unconventional style is filled with grace and acceptance. They do service projects. They take mission trips to foreign countries. They see parts of the United States that they would otherwise never have a chance to see.

Most amazingly, Mike not only talks the talk, but he walks the walk. Mike chose to raise his family right in the heart of North Lawndale. Three adopted kids, and two biological kids. Right in the neighborhood. Not many white families there at all, but Mike Trout, his wife, and his kids are right there, and they have become a major part of the community.

His spirit and enthusiasm, and positive belief in some kids who needed someone to believe in them, have helped an awful lot of young boys become successful men over the years.

He is not famous. And you don't hear much about Mike in papers or magazines or online social media. But that is what the RAH RAH is all about.

Unsung, under the radar, underrated, non-publicized—but doing such outstanding service in the community. There are so many stories like this of people all around our fine world. Makes you feel good amidst the sometimes-depressing news we are inundated with.

A loud RAH RAH for a Real American Hero. Thank you, Mike Trout. (Go to www.YMEN.org for more information.)

If you have any RAH RAH stories or nominations you'd like to let us know about, please email to jcsportsandtees@aol.com, and we will be happy to share all the great stories.

Ponder—Down Yonder

"We often hurt each other
Because we fear each other.
We fear each other
Because we don't know each other."
~Martin Luther King Jr.

You live by the theory of "an eye for an eye"?
Then the whole world ends up being blind.

It is easy to make a buck.
It is much harder to make a difference.

"We are not here for a long time,
We are here for a good time."
~Tim Hagan

Don't wait for the light at the end of the tunnel.
Stride down there and light the bloody thing yourself.

Work like you don't need the money,
Love like you have never been loved,
Dance like nobody's watching,
Sing like nobody's listening,
Live like it is heaven on earth.

The Affliction Known as LOSES

Just wondering if anyone else has come down with this minor "illness."

It is one I have been afflicted with in recent years. I call it LOSES. Acronym for—Lack of Social Endurance Syndrome.

Not exactly life-threatening stuff here, I will admit. But basically, it is a lack of ability to sustain protracted levels of conversation with different people over a long period of time. I'm talking about a crowded room full of people...Like at a party or any social gathering. (Note, I call it LOSES—my wife just calls it being rude.)

Now, I do enjoy social contact and meeting people and catching up with folks I haven't seen for a while—just as much as the next conversationalist. But what I have noticed, lately, is that I hit a certain meltdown point, where the yak-yak shutoff valve just starts to close down.

It's not that the conversation is boring. It's not that I don't enjoy talking to the various people. It's just that the incessant talking and constant conversation becomes suddenly painstakingly slow and difficult to stay with.

Loss of concentration, loss of interest in conversation, minor headache, and general fidgety-ness are the most common symptoms.

My doctor has confirmed none of this can be blamed on an enlarged prostate. Too bad, as I have used that one lately to get out of many an argument and even more household chores.

Sadly, there is no known medicine for this particular ailment. No over-the-counter prescriptions have been shown to help. Medical research remains confounded.

But I have found the best remedy for LOSES is to simply remove yourself from the din of conversation, sit away from the group, and just enjoy some quiet time by yourself while all the yakking continues (note the not-so-subtle anger/jealousy at those who can talk for long periods of time without experiencing any of this localized pain). Another solution I have found is leaving said premises for a nice walk in the fresh air. Sometimes, after a nice twenty-minute walk, the LOSES subsides, and you can rejoin the social group and happily continue with more mundane conversations (again, noting the misplaced anger).

If there are any "LOSES" trained doctors out there who would like to weigh in on this unique "ailment," I would welcome any consultation. Maybe there are others out there who quietly have suffered for years and just needed this pseudo-disease brought out into the public eye.

I would add that the affliction hits usually about an hour and half into the social gathering. Sometimes I can make a "comeback" at a later point, but at other times, once LOSES hits—I am done for the night.

Note: The problem becomes worse if you attend a social gathering with a partner who, unlike you, does love to converse for extended periods of times. (Like say…your wife!)

One final symptom of LOSES: When afflicted, and it is time to leave a party, you pretty much just get up and leave. If you can, giving a quick thank-you and good-bye to the host is nice. But you feel no need whatsoever to go around and say good-bye to the people you have just been talking to for the past few hours.

The theory is, when it is time to leave, just quietly head to the door. Get your coat, and be on your way.

For those who say this is rude and will insult people? In my experience, especially after a few cocktails, nobody will even realize you have gone.

The party goes on. Really.

A Time to Stand and a Time to Think

It is common to almost all sporting events. It is done at the beginning of each of the games. A moment of peace and reflection before a high-energy sporting contest. Anticipation held, momentarily, before the excitement of the contest.

We are not talking about the pregame warmup, or a trip to the concession stands, or even paying for your ticket at the ticket window. No…I speak instead of the playing of our national anthem.

You know the drill. The PA announcer comes on and says, "And now, would you please rise for the playing of our national anthem." Everybody gets quiet and stands up in respect for this sporting tradition. The song is then played either by a tape or the school band, or sung by a guest singer.

It is a wonderful tradition and certainly one that we all follow.

But what are we thinking about as the anthem plays? Standing, and taking the cap off, and crossing your hand across your chest are nice symbolic gestures. But are we really taking in the true meaning of the anthem?

Are we just standing and going through the motions with all of the people next to us? Or are we taking that time, while the music is playing—in our own personal way—to honor our country and be thankful for all that we've been given.

For instance…as the anthem is playing, are we thinking about the fact that there really were people—real people, not just figures we read about in history books or watched movies about on TV, who risked their lives and had the incredible foresight and bravery to come to America and help to create the many fruits that we now bear?

As the music is playing, are we thinking about the fact that there are, sure as we are standing here right now, American military personnel stationed overseas whose very lives are being risked every day, so that again we can enjoy a safe environment here in the States? As you stare at the flag, try to imagine what it must be like. Young kids…trying to be brave, trying to be strong, but still human and, I am sure, at least at times, very scared. As I listen to the anthem, I try to think of their fear and quietly, in my head, thank them for hanging in there.

Most of all, as we stand in pride, I like to think of all the things I am thankful for. Good health, family, friends, and the means to enjoy them comfortably. And more importantly, how we can help others to enjoy the same.

Finally, I will at times think about how lucky we are to enjoy each and every sports event we attend.

What a thrill it is to be part of athletic competition, with all its emotion and spirit and enthusiasm. Talented athletes performing in an atmosphere of intensity and great competitiveness. The crowd…the band…the players. The coaches. I never want to take that for granted, and the sixty seconds while the national anthem is playing is a good time to remind myself of just that.

So again, standing and taking your hat off are nice gestures to show respect to our national anthem. But some in-depth thinking might be an even better salute to our country. Looking at the flag and really appreciating what it stands for might be the best sign of respect we could give.

Francis Scott Key would be proud, I think, if we did just that.

And it does help put the competition we are about to see in perspective.

Suddenly our team winning or losing doesn't become all that important. Life will go on in both victory and defeat.

Now, when the anthem is over, go ahead and get loud, get rowdy, and cheer on your favorite team!

Shake Up Sunday Morning TV

This one started out as somewhat of a joke, but the more I thought about it, if given the proper production and direction, I think this could work.

Here's the idea.

You know all the Sunday morning news shows that have been on forever? *Meet the Press, Face the Nation, The Week in Review*, etc. They have been Sunday morning fixtures since Dan Rather was a young man—or the invention of the TV—I am not sure which one came first. But you get the picture.

And they are all well-done, informational programs. A variety of guests and opinions. Quality hosts. No problems here at all.

Here is my idea to counter some of those shows. Time to throw a little curveball into Sunday morning news television.

How about something like this? And we might have to go to cable with this one. Let's call it *Meet the Streets—The Sunday Not-So-News Conference.*

Here's the idea. My panel will be made up of four or five folks who have been out on the streets, either currently homeless, have been homeless in the past, or others who have experienced or are experiencing some of the real hardships of life.

It could be a different four or five people each week. But always representative of that group. The host would need a particularly unique brand of skills including being informative, inquiring, sympathetic, and a sense of humor with just a slight dash of real unbridled, raging anger thrown in just for kicks.

I would nominate myself first. But if salary negotiations break down, or the background check thing doesn't go so well…I would settle on a Jon Stewart or maybe a Robin Roberts as the host.

But here is the idea...

I have spent some time recently working at the front desk of a homeless assistance shelter called Connections—located in Evanston, Illinois. They house and provide a multitude of services for those who are or have been struggling with homelessness. Great place. Wonderful and caring staff.

I have, over the past few years, been able to meet and get to know many of the clients. I talk to them and hear their stories, and situations, and struggles. Most are pretty realistic about their current situation.

What I have found is this. Actually three things: 1) There are some awfully colorful and interesting personalities among the group. Many are outgoing, honest, and full of humor and spirit; 2) they have a story to tell. The incredible insight and knowledge they possess of what it's like living in such a tough situation on a daily basis, many times out on the streets for long periods of time, provides tremendous insight on how we might help. Listening to and understanding the multitude of hurdles many of them have to overcome to get themselves out of their current difficulties is truly eye-opening; 3) we could learn much from the suggestions, ideas, and intelligence they offer, including clear, real, and specific examples of things that could improve the situation they are in.

With the unfiltered color and communication styles of our panel, I am certain it would be an outstanding watch. I think it could be extremely informational and educational and definitely entertaining!

What a contrast this would be to the other Sunday morning news shows. Dare I say, you would be able to learn just as much from this show as from the "panel of high-ranking experts" on the major news shows?

Just picture for a few seconds the *Meet the Press* panel. Let that vision set in. Now picture our *Meet the Streets* panel. No wardrobe changes, no TV makeup. You get them as they are. Now go back to

Meet the Press for a second. Now picture our *Meet the Streets* panel again. You get the idea.

My plan would be to make this show completely unscripted (thus the need for cable) with the moderator having certain preplanned questions, but letting the panel go mostly freelance.

Talk about a stark difference! I think Sunday viewers would welcome our presence.

If not Roberts or Stewart to run the show, how about Will Smith, Rapper "Killer Mike" (seriously), Bill Maher, Stephen Colbert, or the wonderfully disheveled Chris Matthews. Plenty of candidates to host. And again if we can't get anybody to take on the project…well, then, hand me the microphone and let's roll.

Think Tank

When you play—play hard.
When you work—don't play.

Remember (and this applies to work relationships as well as
arguments with loved ones),
the bamboo that bends is stronger than the sturdy oak that resists.

"If everyone demanded peace instead of another television set:
Then there would be peace."
~John Lennon
From United Press International

There is only one place where you begin at the top,
And that is when you are digging a hole.

In golf, the reason the teaching pro tells you
to keep your head down
is so you won't look up and see him laughing.

Sign seen at a beach:
WILL SWIM FOR FOOD

Jon Cohn

Sign seen at forest preserve entrance:
NO SWIMMING, NO PICNICKING, NO HUNTING, NO CAMPING,
NO FIRES, NO BALL THROWING, NO SHOWERS, NO MUSIC,
NO LOUD TALKING, NO BOATING...HAVE FUN!

Sign seen at tennis court:
LOVE—MEANS NOTHING.

The 7 Pillars of Personal Greatness
(by Robert H. Cohn)

COMPASSION
Conscious of distress in others, together with a desire to alleviate it.

CHARITY
Kindness of help for the needy or suffering.

INTEGRITY
Adherence to a code of moral, artistic, or other values.

HONESTY
A refusal to lie, steal, or deceive in any way.

TRUSTWORTHINESS
Worthy of confidence. Dependable.

LOYALTY
Faithful to a person, cause, ideal, or custom.

SELF-RESPECT
A high or special regard for oneself (but not overly so).

Sins and Grins

"Life is not measured by the number of breaths we take,
but by the moments that take our breath away."
(If you do not pass this on to at least eight people…who cares?)
~George Carlin

"Statistics are like bikinis. They show a lot. But not everything."
~Lou Piniella
Baseball Manager

"I am writing a book. So far I have all the page numbers done."
~Steven Wright

Reality is just a crutch for people who can't handle drugs.

A man read that most accidents occur within
two miles of your home.
So he moved.

Then there is the story about the guy who painted
a giant blue square in his backyard
just to trick people viewing Google Earth
into thinking that he had a swimming pool.

How come they haven't found a cure yet
for death by natural causes?

I hate noise on planes.
Especially explosions.

College Overrated? You Bet Your Sweet Bippy!

Note that the title here does not say useless, or bad, or insignificant. Not at all. Just *overrated*.

Here are some of my observations of the overration of college life, and believe me, you won't find this advice in any of the "How to find the right college for your child" handbooks.

Okay, here we go…

1. The battle to go upwardly mobile to get into the most "prestigious" or high-ranking university is a complete, or near-complete, waste of time. Reputation is all it is. Any company hiring you out of school just because of what school you graduated from, and not the experience you have or the personality and character you bring to the table, is a company you probably don't want to work for anyway.

Bottom line here: You can go to any school in the country and work hard and get yourself a good education. You can also go to any school in the country and completely blow it off and party your soul away. Doesn't matter if you're at Harvard or Okawville Junior College. You get out of it what you put into it. So forget how the school is "rated or ranked," and pick the best fit for you.

2. Understand—and most first-time tuition-paying parents don't—that your student will be taught by mostly grad students and teaching assistants during the first two years of their academic experience.

So, to be clear...for your $20,000 or $30,000 tuition fee, your idealistic young student sent off into the throes of academia for the first time, is being taught by young first-time teachers who have *never* been trained to teach. They may know the subject. But that doesn't mean they are good teachers. Can't tell you how many times I heard from my own kids, and others, how the teachers in high school knew "how to teach" better than their college teach- ers. They definitely don't tell you about these grad students as "teacher/professors" in all the lovely college brochures.

Note: If you know this going in, and if you know it while you are nervously penning your first tuition check, then fine, *no problemo*— you go into it with open eyes. But I would argue that too many par- ents just go with the flow, and don't realize their young college student is being taught by young college grad students until after a couple of semesters' worth of checks have been deposited. By then, there may be no turning back.

3.   Now, here's the kicker! After two years with these inexperienced teaching assistants, your child will finally be taking some advanced—call them "meat and potatoes"—classes. Finally! They will be taught often by very experienced, well-qualified older pro- fessors. *But*...and again, you won't find this info in your friendly neighborhood college brochure...most of these older professors really don't put a priority on teaching their classes. Instead, their emphasis is on research. And getting published. Not on teaching your son or daughter's class. So after finally waiting

for two years to get to the really qualified expert professors...you often find out these professors would
rather be anywhere but in the classroom teaching!

Again, to emphasize my point—the professors in college get paid
and the college's reputation is based, not on these professor's teaching
ability, but instead on how many degrees they have, how advanced
is their education, and how much their research gets published. Not
on how well they teach the class! Aren't you paying those exorbitant
college tuition fees so your child can get the best teaching possible?
But, as you can see, the lines don't always connect here. And my biggest issue is that so many parents do not become aware of this until
after the fact.

So...to sum this little portion up, you are paying thousands of
dollars for a college education taught by, in the first two years, potentially non-qualified young grad students, and in the final two years,
by professors who may be qualified, but whose interest and emphasis
often lie elsewhere.

Sorry to be an upper-education downer here. And, of course,
there are many exceptions where fine teaching takes place. But, more
often than not, the picture I have painted is all too real.

Now, we are not done yet on my somewhat blindsided attack
on upper education (my doctoral-educated wife is going to kill me).
And I do understand I'm emphasizing the dark side here probably
way too much—things certainly are not always this negative—but
what the heck? I'm on a roll here, so I might as well keep trying to
make the point.

For the reader, this might be a good time in my college non-
dissertation rant to take a nice break. If you need a glass of water, or
possibly something stronger (Jägermeister might work well with the
next few points), now would be an excellent time to go get one.

But return to this point ready to keep rolling. Please.

4. Have you noticed the incredible amount of mailings and college recruitment notices you get starting
in your late sophomore year and ending near May
of your high school senior season? "We really want
Johnny, or Suzy, to come to (insert overpriced school
name here), our school." Or something like… "Why
Missouri Institute of Design and Technology is the
right school for you!"

All of these mailings come complete with incredibly beautiful brochures, complete with fancy graphics and designs. Not only do they
sound good…but they look gorgeous. At one point, I was tempted to
apply myself. I had my application ready to go to Upper Montana State
of the Scenic Mountains. (Good old UMSOTSM!) It looked so nice,
the scenery so beautiful and luscious. I had my application all set (fifty-
nine-year-old…looking for better life…interested in majoring in high
altitude meditation).

But, of course, I don't need to tell you that the colleges that send
out these beautiful brochures with personal letters have no idea who
your "Johnny or Suzy" really is. They simply are trying to get students
to come to their school.

The reason?

These colleges make money. And they need your tuition money to
keep it going! They often prey on the parents and students, and they
do this by sending these enticing and beautifully designed brochures—
falsely personalized, of course!

Understand this: In order for the professors to make their salaries.
And for the administrators to make theirs. And for the guidance coun-
selors to make theirs. And for the school president, and vice president, and provost (what is a provost anyways?) to make their money

and receive their complimentary car, complimentary house, complimentary housekeeping, and complimentary mint on their pillow each night—they need your tuition money! It's as simple as that.

4.5) Just as a side note, and to add salt to the already academically infected wound, many colleges are now rated by the percentage of applicants that they turn away! That's right, they are recruiting all these young students in a large part so they get a large applicant pool and then send your kid a rejection notice. They can then boast that "we only accept 14 percent of the people who apply," and get ranked higher because of that low percentage…. As my grandfather used to say, "Put that in your pipe and smoke it."

5. Books! The price of the textbooks for college? Off the charts. Nearly criminal. Half the time your student buys the books, and the teacher never even requires them to be used for the class. Too painful to discuss. Next!

6. Often in the first two years, students will be taking classes similar in material and difficulty to their high school classes. Kids and parents get all excited about potentially unique and interesting subjects they can study in college, only to find out the first two years they have to take required classes that are similar to those they took in high school…. Yep. Got to get those dreaded "Gen Ed" classes in.

7. It goes without saying that while they are away at college and enjoying first-time independence, the top priority for your fine young student will not necessarily be academic based. Getting comfortable so-

cially and making new friends in college also means partying, drinking, and general decadent revelry.

That's not to say they won't concentrate on academics some and hopefully get involved in some worthwhile clubs…but especially during the first two years, it's all about staying up late, making new friends, drinking, and socializing to the extreme—whatever that might involve.

Nothing wrong with this. It is part of growing up. But again, you are paying $30,000 for this freedom to party. Just a friendly reminder.

In junior and senior year, the novelty wears off some, and many of the kids do get more serious. The partying then may take a backseat. A little bit. But the first two years? Just sowing the wild oats. Again, remember your paying the same tuition every year!

So…in conclusion…

I probably have been way too hard on the world of academia at the collegiate level. There are, of course, many, many wonderful benefits. And it can be a great and developing four years for any young man or woman. I understand that.

But the reason I go overboard some in my criticism, is that I see way too many—I mean, *way* too many parents and kids—getting on what I call the college treadmill. Just get on the track and try to keep up with everybody else. Follow what everyone else is doing. But too often we follow this path, I would argue, without critically thinking—is college really the right decision?

Will your son or daughter best benefit from going to college for four years? And, if so, will he or she go to the best school for him or her or the school with the best reputation?

Right now in many high schools, and in many family rooms across America, they are not asking *whether or not* you should you go to college; they are asking *where*, just assuming you are going.

And that I think is wrong!

Final thought: A good solid compromise solution that more and more people are starting to figure out? Go to a junior college for two years and get your basic classes out of the way without spending thousands of dollars. Maybe get a job while you are in junior college, thus gaining some valuable work experience—as well as making a little bit of money. Then you have your feet on the ground and a much better level of maturity in order to choose which university to attend.

You end up paying two years' tuition instead of four. (Wow! College loans could be paid back before you reach your mid-forties!) And you still have a degree from whatever four-year institution you choose.

My Philosophy (on School) Summed Up Distinctly

"Never let school get in the way of your education."

And Speaking of Degrees

It probably wouldn't surprise you at this point to tell you I have never been overly impressed with academic "degrees."

Now, I fully respect the hard work and dedication it takes to get a master's degree, or a doctorate. Tremendous accomplishment, no doubt.

But I also equally fully respect the worker who has been a garbage collector for ten years, doing his job diligently and faithfully. And I fully respect the waiter or waitress who has been faithfully fulfilling their duties at a restaurant for a long period of time. Or the truck driver with a long time with the same company and a good, honest driving record.

None of them have "degrees," but they all get my utmost admiration.

Why should we call those with advanced degrees "Dr.", but not give any special designation for those who have served well in hard working labor-type jobs for many years?

Again, this is no disrespect for the hard earned academic work of so many, but instead equal respect for those who worked at other jobs that didn't include advanced schooling

In short, if I could bring it down to a level where I probably shouldn't, I could sum up my philosophy on higher education like this:

"I am not overly impressed with degrees. A thermometer has degrees. And you know what a nurse does with a thermometer."

"Sign" of the Times

Sign seen outside local bar:
"Free Beer…Tomorrow"

Or better yet…

A rock band decided to call itself "Free Beer"—
that way when the sign says "Free Beer at 9 Tonight,"
they will be guaranteed to have a big crowd!

Instead of complaining that the world is a very cold place…
go build a bunch of small fires.

"I can live with those who may hate or dislike me,
But I cannot live with those who do agree,
but say nothing or remain silent."
~Martin Luther King Jr.

I am now getting much better at multitasking.
I can actually ignore more than one thing at a time.

What if birds are not really singing?
Maybe they are screaming because they're afraid of heights.

I dig, you dig, we dig, and they dig.
It is not much of a poem, but it is pretty deep.

Makes Sense?

"I don't have any fear of death.
My only fear is to come back reincarnated."
~Tupac Shakur

A young man's boss gave him this advice:
Dress for the job you want, not the job you have.
He then spent the next day in a disciplinary meeting after
wearing a Batman outfit to work.

The only place where *success* comes before *work*
is in the dictionary.

Every little bit matters. Every small thing counts.
Each person in a group or team is crucial.
We call this the Umbrella Effect.
Think of an umbrella with a small hole at the top.
When it starts to rain hard,
99 percent of the umbrella is in fine functioning shape.
But 1 percent (the small hole at the top) is not.
And when it rains hard and you are
holding that umbrella over your head,
you are indeed getting very, very wet.

Seen on the front of a soccer player's shirt:
"Never go through life without goals."

Comedy Central

My brother-in-law died recently.
He was a karate expert who joined the army.
The first time he saluted, he killed himself.

Always borrow from a pessimist,
because they never expect to get it back.

There is the story of the guy who was so lazy
he wouldn't even walk down the path of least resistance.

If life is a waste of time,
And time is a waste of life,
Then let's all get wasted together
And have the time of our lives.

Think about this:
The optimist proclaims that we live in the best
of all possible worlds;
the pessimists fears this is true.

Drugs may lead nowhere,
but it is quite the scenic route.

Two Different Thought Processes

find it interesting, when it comes to the vast income inequality we see in our country today, that there really are two different reactions. Two completely different views that folks seem to have.

There are those people who are legitimately disturbed by the tremendous difference in incomes and lifestyles. These people are innately bothered by the fact that no matter how talented, or how hard someone worked to achieve financial success, some people in our society are able to make millions of dollars and additionally gain work bonuses, contract buyouts and contract incentives like paid-for cars, travel, etc.—while many others toil in near poverty, scraping to get by.

The other point of view looks at the great success stories of people who have built up enormous wealth and cite this as an example of what is great about America. They are not bothered by the income difference, and they look at the wealthy as shining examples of what we all might accomplish by striving for...the American Dream, if you will.

Now, the common reaction after reading the above descriptions is "why can't we believe in both?" And the answer is you can. Maybe.

The common and reasonable explanation many people have is that we would like to see more people on the lower, struggling end get help and work their way up to middle class, while not limiting the amount people can make at the top end.

Okay. That is possible. And we can roll with that if you would like.

But I am more interested here in the internal reaction people have to the differences stated above.

Let's put it another way. When people hear of a sports star signing a contract for, say, $63 million for four years, or a movie star getting $90 million to make a movie (plus residuals! I'm not sure what "residuals" you need when you're already getting $90 million, but hey, go for it if you can), you can expect two different reactions from people.

Most seem to say, wow, good for him (or her…no, wait…not her, as unfortunately not many "hers" are getting that kind of money). Let him get all he can get if management is willing to pay and the market is there. It's free enterprise at its best. Good for him!

Others, and it seems to be a depressingly small minority, are bothered, if not disgusted, by the amount of the contract. They feel that no matter how talented, and no matter what the market decides it can bear—it is simply not morally right for someone to be getting that much money.

So interestingly, some us accept the fact—even revel in it—that certain people in our society can make multimillions. Others find it quite disturbing.

Two totally different mind-sets and internal character thermometers.

I am not afraid in the least to say how I personally feel here, not being a big fan of political correctness myself.

Here is how I look at it:

The vast income inequality in today's society bothers the hell out of me. And when I hear of multimillion-dollar contracts for movie stars, athletes, and top executives, and then hear about, or meet, so many others who work so hard, still have so little, and struggle just to get by…well, it drives a drill right into my gut, and the painful drilling doesn't stop till it hits somewhere down near the bottom—right about at pure disgust.

And, quite frankly, I am amazed more people don't share this disgust.

Again, nothing wrong with working hard and making money, and getting your just rewards for your hard work and success.

It is the revolting excess that is so deeply bothersome.

But…

On the Other Hand

am a strong, strong believer that income inequality in today's society is a big problem, but…

One thing liberals never mention enough, and sometimes forget in their occasional attempts to defrock the top 1 percent?

The incredible amount of charitable money that has been given by these folks.

Almost without exception, those of great wealth have been tremendously giving with their money to so many wonderful causes.

It bears worth knowing and understanding that many organizations and many needy or sick people have been helped tremendously over so many years by the large amount of contributions given by these generous folks.

Real differences have been made from this philanthropic giving.

Liberals, in all of their very legitimate arguments and differences with "the 1 percent," simply do not bring this fact up enough.

Jon Cohn

Laugh Trax

"The upper crust is just a bunch of crumbs held together by dough."
~Joseph A. Thomas

A man explaining the secret to making a marriage last:
Two times a week we go out. We go to a nice restaurant,
have a little wine, a little food…
she goes Tuesdays and I go Fridays.

Heard from a man on the streets:
"I started out with absolutely nothing…and I still have most of it!"

After his team lost 51-0, a coach was asked
what he thought about the execution of his team.
"I'm all for it," he said.

"I always take life with a grain of salt
…and a slice of lemon…and a shot of tequila."
~Jimmy Buffett

From a diary somewhere…
I want to die peacefully in my sleep like my grandfather,
Not screaming and yelling like the passengers in his car.

Extended Laugh Trax

*A*little old man shuffled very slowly into an ice cream parlor. He pulled himself up very slowly and exceedingly painfully, and after much struggle, finally made it up onto the stool. After catching his breath, he ordered a banana split.

The waitress asked kindly, "Crushed nuts?"

"No," he replied. "Arthritis."

What Have They Done to Birthday Cake?

ake. It is called birthday *cake*.

Would somebody please bring back the "cake" in the good, old-fashioned birthday cake?

Have you seen and/or tasted the birthday cakes of late? They are basically delivering frosting, with slivers of cake thrown in between.

What happened to the cake part? I used to love a little bit of frosting layer on my cake. It was a thin layer and there was not much of it. So the frosting was really special. It was a treat to get to that part.

Now?

Holy cow! The sliver has turned to slather. The cake has become thick frosting infested in all crevices. Excuse me...would you like to have some cake with your frosting?

The last few years the birthday cakes I have had at kids' parties (I'm slightly worried after writing this book that my invitation list may go down exceedingly) have been generally layered as follows: heavy frosting on the outside...thin cake layer...medium layer of frosting...thin layer of cake...another medium layer of frosting...a bit more cake...and then, *presto!* Another big layer of frosting on the outside!

What happened to the cake part!

I used to lick the frosting because there was so little of it, and it tasted so sugary good. Now I treat myself by just licking the few pieces of actual cake that I can find between the forests of frosting. (Not, by the way, necessarily a good look. And one definitely to get you some uncomfortable stares from a not-so-amused group of seven-year-olds.)

And the colored frosting? What exactly is it made of? Last time my tongue stayed multicolored for days before I finally had to "Shout it out" with some extra-powerful stain remover. Which wasn't bad-tasting, actually, but it did give me a strange desire to go outside on the lawn and tumble dry on a low setting.

My perfect dessert cake? Glad you asked.

A giant piece of chocolate cake—but *only* the cake part. No frosting. Just the cake. In a big bowl. Pour milk over the cake. Use spoon to re-drench the cake with milk as you go.

Now that's what I'm talking about. Heaven, absolute heaven.

What Are We Thinking About Here?

Found it kind of odd the other day, when going to work out at the local fitness center, to see two perfectly healthy, perfectly able-bodied young men walking into the elevator.

The elevator...the fitness center was on the second floor!

So...let me ponder this for just a moment... You're going to get in a workout, and you can't take one flight of stairs up? You had to use the elevator instead?

While on the topic...

What is with the people who get all upset when you don't park in the "closest available" parking spot at a shopping center, grocery store, entertainment complex, or the like?

If you pass a spot or two and God forbid park five or six spots farther away from the store, it's as if you have committed a mortal sin. I don't get it. What is the big deal? Maybe we could get an elevator to take these exercise-fearing folks straight into the store.

REALLY?

Nothing major here, but there is something wrong about this picture.

I recently observed a nice man and woman taking a carriage ride through the streets of Chicago on a beautiful and unseasonably warm December night. It was the absolute perfect scene for a romantic carriage ride. Everybody out and about doing their Christmas shopping...Christmas music playing...all the stars clear and crisp on this wonderful winter night.

But...both of them were sitting in the carriage pounding away on their iPhones. Heads down, entrenched in their ever-expanding data minutes. While riding in the carriage!

Folks, you paid $75 for the carriage ride! On this perfect night!

If ever there was time to put away the cell phone and just watch the night pass by, this was it!

The Older I Get,
The Smarter My Parents Get

I am sure you've heard this old expression.

But it came back to me recently as I was engrossed in yet another television episode of "up close and personal" on Animal Planet.

Now, sometimes they catch the animals in the act being a little *too* personal—but hey, natural habitat is natural habitat, right?

I used to observe my dad watch these shows and wonder what was so interesting about just watching animals in the forest. Sounded boring to me. And I wanted the TV back so I could watch any of my favorite cowboy shows when I was a kid. (*Gunsmoke, The Lone Ranger,* and *The Gene Autry Show* were my top three.)

But, now, presto! Some forty years later, I, like my dad back in the day, have become a huge fan!

Have you watched one of these shows lately? It is unbelievable how they capture the sights, sounds, and scenery of the animal kingdom. Amazing film work and production.

Doesn't matter if they are following insects, fish, small animals such as badgers or raccoons, or the "big boys" like bears, giraffes, or gorillas—the filming is amazing, and the fact that we can now see it all in clear, picturesque HD makes it that much better.

It's so cool to watch and see. It's fascinating to observe the animals. And it makes you appreciate that they, like us humans, are all part of whatever this universe and life is all about.

But, of course, my kids now feel the same way as I did when I was young. They see me watching these shows and wonder what I see in them. Yep. Life does, indeed, come full circle.

Barack's First Bad Step

was a huge fan, and still am, of President Obama. His coming-of-age as a young Chicago politician to being elected president of the United States in such a brief amount of time was both incredible and inspirational.

Even more important and inspirational were the messages he gave to our country as he was campaigning. Wonderfully inspiring. Therapy for the soul. And much needed for our country at the time, I thought.

While I still think he has been a great president and I deeply respect the character and intelligence of the man, we all know by now that his first-term presidency did not turn out quite as positive as we might have originally thought. The first four years he made some mistakes, had to compromise often, and of course had to deal with some of the stark realities of the political world.

His idealism and positive mojo took a bit of a hit—none more indicative than the graying of his hair almost right before our eyes.

But I go back to an early key decision he made, which to me signified the beginning of the downfall of his true liberal and inspiring agenda during those first four years (an agenda that I still believe in, by the way, and that came to fruition in a large part in his second term).

In my opinion, this was Barack's first mistake as president.

The decision was about where his young daughters would go to school. Malia and Sasha were about nine and twelve at the time. And the Obamas were moving to Washington, D.C., so obviously new schools would have to be chosen.

When it came to deciding, instead of choosing to enroll them at one of the city's struggling public schools…they decided to enroll the girls at a top-end private school.

An understandable decision, for sure. But I thought an unfortunate one.

Yes, he was the president now. But he had just finished campaigning on a platform of raising and uplifting the lower and middle classes. His pledge to trying to minimize the income and opportunity inequality in this country was spot-on. He spoke eloquently of better opportunities for those among us who might not have as much.

So, what a wonderful and symbolic statement it would have been for him and Michelle to send their daughters to the local public school. What a message that would have sent! It would have been both symbolic and real! I believe it would have set the tone for his entire presidency.

"If it is not good enough for my daughters, then it is not good enough. And we need to change it so that it is," could have been his message. It would have signaled to the disadvantaged that yes, we truly have a president who is different and will do more than talk, but he will live with us and try to make things better.

Again, it was a small and mostly unrecognized decision. But to me, the sending of his kids to private school was the first step in the wrong direction for our fine liberal and activist president. Maybe not so much for what it was—but for what it could have been.

As our guy Martin Luther King Jr. once famously said, "What happens to the least of us in this country, happens to all of us."

To his credit, Obama lived to that creed every day of his presidency.

My Favorite Will

Heard a comedian once say that he really doesn't like his kids that much. So...in his will he is going to state, "Whatever is left over after the funeral, I give to my children."

But then he goes on to say, "And then I am going to go out and have the biggest, most expensive funeral you could possibly have!"

It Is Rough Getting Old

A couple in their nineties are both have trouble remembering things. During a checkup the doctor tells them they might want to start writing things down to help them remember.

Later that night while watching TV, the old man gets up from his chair. "You want anything while I am in the kitchen?" he asks.

"Will you get me a bowl of ice cream?"

"Sure," he says.

"Don't you think you should write it down so you can remember it?" she asks.

"No, I can remember it."

"Well, I would like some strawberries on top, too. Maybe you should write that down so as not to forget it."

He says, "No, I can remember that. You want a bowl of ice cream with strawberries on top."

"I'd also like whipped cream. I am certain you will forget that. Write it down," she says.

Irritated, he says, "I don't need to write it down, I can remember it! Ice cream with strawberries and whipped cream—I got it, for goodness' sake!"

Then he toddles into the kitchen. After about twenty minutes, the old man returns from the kitchen and hands his wife a plate of bacon and eggs. She stares at the plate for a moment and says, "Hey, where's my toast?"

Longtime Love Affair with the Snooze Alarm

Nobody is a bigger fan of the good old-fashioned snooze alarm than I. For some very odd and unexplained reason, I enjoy waking up extra early to the sound of the beautiful buzzing of the snooze alarm.

I will hit that puppy sometimes five, six, seven times on any given morning. My college roommate used to say it sounded like World War II in our room with all the noise.

See, I have no problem getting back to sleep. That is the key. So in my very weird, and somewhat dilapidated thinking, I like to wake up, so I then can enjoy being able to go back to sleep!

You see, the theory is, if I am sleeping then I can't enjoy being able to sleep. I am unconscious. But if I wake up and realize I can go back to sleep, then I have the enjoyment of knowing I can sleep some more.

This is seriously deranged thinking, I know…but—

To me it makes perfect sense. To absolutely no one but me.

Psychologists have analyzed this and concluded that I have some undetected personality disorder. Their recommendations to me were to 1) stay away from sharp objects, and 2) whatever I do, never write about this in a book!

Oh, and waking up to music or other soothing sounds they have out there now? That's just weak… I mean, c'mon, be a man! You gotta go with the good old-fashioned buzzer sound—none of this soft music stuff. Use the ten-minute delay. Not nine. Not eleven. Ten. Old school, baby, old school.

As a master snooze-alarmist I also have different shut-off techniques. I offer these as a service to any young snooze alarm enthusiast out there who might want to add some variety to their morning routine.

From being sound asleep, to be woken by the alarm, there are different methods that can be used to get that delightful extra ten minutes. These are a few I have developed after many years of hard work and experience:

1. The "quick jab." Near arm. Quick fist bump to shut off alarm. Effective, but not much for style points. Good starting point for all the young kids out there.

2. The "quick tap slap." Degree of difficulty about 6.5. Must elevate the near arm from the bed. With eyes closed and arm at high raised position, then point index finger downward and descend quickly. Index finger lands direct hit on snooze alarm and you're good for ten more minutes. With practice, even with eyes closed you can get dead-on accuracy here…. This can be fun for the whole family.

3. The "typewriter technique." Normally only seen in Midwestern states. Involves a semi trance–like fumbling of the fingers trying to find the correct button to shut alarm off. You're still 75 percent asleep, but all five fingers, thumb included, are involved in this tricky but effective multi-tap excursion, thus the typewriter comparison. Positives: With five fingers searching you should quickly find the right button and snooze away for ten more minutes. Negatives: You have probably hit so many incorrect buttons that the time on your clock is now three hours off, and when you turn the radio on, you may be listening to the religious stylings of the Mormon Tabernacle Choir.

4. The "crossover reverse slam." This one is good. Really good. Simple, but impressively effective. Take far arm (without disturbing person immediately adjacent) and reach across the body with a full swing jab at the snooze button. It will take extended hours of practice to hit the "bull's-eye," but once mastered, it will be well worth the wait. For best style points go quickly and with strong authority. This move can be dangerous, and should only be done in the privacy of your own home. Or...try it at a party and impress your friends!

So there you have it. Everything you ever wanted to know about the snooze alarm, and probably a whole lot you didn't want to learn.

Whatever your reasons for buying this book, I'm quite sure it wasn't to learn about the inside intricacies of the snooze alarm.

But I just couldn't resist giving a little love to my dear longtime companion.

Cell phones and other technology have replaced the good old clock radio.

I know it is a dying breed, and our time together may not be long. So this segment was dedicated to you.

Rest well, clock radio. Rest well.

The Ultimate Optimistic Thought

Can't think of anyone who ever had a more optimistic outlook than this guy.

Doctor tells him if he continues to drink and smoke as much as he currently does, he very likely could take ten to fifteen years off of his life expectancy. The optimistic young man then tells the doctor, "Well, look at the bright side! If it does happen, I will have ten to fifteen more years of death!"

Religion—Thought Number One

I was sitting in church the other day. Keep in mind I am technically Jewish, but I married into a Catholic family, so I have attended church many times over the years and always enjoy the experience, which I will explain later.

I often like to observe the people in the church. But maybe this particular time, even more than usual.

I study attention levels, body language, eye contact, and general disposition of people sitting in the pews, then standing during the service. Obviously, this is not a perfect science. It is only a personal observation. But I do believe you can read a lot about a person by observing these things closely…and I actually think I might be pretty good at it, as well.

Here is what I saw…

If I had to roughly judge what percentage of the people at the service were really into it, versus the people who appeared to be there only in body…but not necessarily in true spirit? I would say maybe 25 percent. On my observation, only a small portion find the depth and meaning of the service and the homily.

The others, to me, looked like they were partially into it. Some just fulfilling their duty. They were there. But they really weren't there, if you know what I mean.

To me, if you are going to attend a particular service and make this part of your weekly ritual, it should be because you truly are into it. Goes back to the good old MBHS we have talked about: Mind, Body, Heart, and Soul.

Again, just my opinion, but if you are going to go to a church or any kind of religious service on a regular basis, it should be because you believe strongly. You are committed and fully entrenched in the message and spirit of what is going on in the church. It should not, as I observe all too often, be because that's what your parents did and you feel you should do the same with your kids.

If you are not really into the religion, and don't really believe in the message and formality of the services, maybe your time would be better served by spending the day with your kids doing some service-related project, or helping a needy or worthy organization?

Just a thought.

I have always felt that if there is a God out there, or some "superior" being, he would much rather have me working for a good cause, or some worthwhile project for a couple hours on Sunday, than to have me inside listening to a ceremony that I am only attending for methodical, ritualistic, guilt-laden reasons.

Having said that, and I contradict myself somewhat here, I enjoy going to church. Despite not being Catholic and not following or believing in much of the history and traditions of the Catholic religion, I do enjoy the solitude...the music...the peacefulness...and it does allow me some wonderful quiet thinking time, taking myself away from my daily routines and tasks, and helping me to remember the things that are so much more important in life.

Whether it is inside a church on Sunday mornings, or at a different place of your choosing—I do think finding time for this reflection is important for all of us.

And if church serves that purpose, then that alone is reason enough for its value.

On a Related Thought

Hands that are busy, are holier than lips that pray.

The slightest bit of good is better than the best of intentions.

It is better to light one candle, than to curse the darkness.

Never underestimate the importance of small tasks. Remember:
Little things are the hinges upon which great things occur.

Nothing is so tiring as small tasks left undone.

Don't count the days, make the days count.

Sign seen at a local church:
"Praise be the Lord. Lift your spirit to Jesus.
Reminder: Bingo this Tuesday."

Whoever said nothing is impossible
never tried slamming shut a revolving door.

This Is Really a Club?

O n a recent warm weather vacation, I settled down for a nice comfy read with the local paper and was amused, to say the least, by this front page story and accompanying picture: "Southwest Florida, Gulf Coast Polar Plunge Club, makes annual dip into water."

The picture shows hundreds of "brave?" Florida polar plungers running en masse from the beach to take a December dip into the Gulf of Mexico.

On second look and thought, my mild amusement turned to mid-range-decibel laughter.

Sixty degrees outside, and they are taking their "Polar Plunge"? Midwesterners and East Coasters alike have to be amused by that one.

Now, living in Chicago, or New York, or Boston—in the middle of winter—those "Polar Plunges" are *really* polar plunges. We're talking serious stuff here.

You take your clothes off in January and jump into the cold Lake Michigan waters? That, my friendly readers, is bravery beyond the call of duty. And, of course, it is all for a good cause. (At least I *hope* it is for a good cause!)

I have worked at many of these Polar Plunges over the years. The one I have been most involved in raises money for the local Special Olympics organization, a wonderful group with an equally wonderful mission.

But I get the easy job. I am the announcer and/or emcee. I don't have to jump in. I get all the fun of the Polar Plunge festivities without the shock and awe of the actual frigid dip. Easy for me. All the credit in the world goes to the well-meaning and gutsy participants who raise money for their "dip" into the frigid waters.

But back to our "Polar Plungers"…in Florida? Really? Florida? A "Polar" Plunge?

Sorry, but to borrow a line from our trucker friends back in the days of CB radios: "That's a negatory—ten-four."

Now, you want to impress us, Floridians? You want to match our Polar Plunge events up here in the East and Midwest?

How about this sadistic idea?

Take a mid-July day in Florida. Say, a balmy 105 degrees and humid. Have everyone dress up in jackets, long pants, and wool socks. Have them all gather on the beach. And then have everyone run through a set of hot coals, followed by a sprint through a football field–length fire pit built on both sides—avoiding the fire, while dripping in sweat from the combo of heavy clothing and deathly Florida heat and humidity?

Now, that would be impressive!

Instead of the "Polar Plunge," you could call it the "Florida Fire Fry." Imagine the fun and enjoyment. And please feel free to raise money for a good cause of your choice!

Oh, and if you need an emcee for the event—I will be happy to pitch in! All expenses paid, of course. And I get to wear shorts and a Hawaiian shirt of my own choosing.

Sound good? Beautiful. Have your people contact my people and they can do lunch.

Simple Wisdom...Simply the Best Kind

From *All I Really Need to Know I Learned in Kindergarten*
by Robert Fulghum

"All I really need to know about how to live and what to do and how to be, I learned in kindergarten. Wisdom was not at the top of the graduate school mountain, but there in the sandpile at school. These are the things I learned:

"*Share everything *Play fair *Don't hit people *Put things back where you found them *Clean up your own mess *Don't take things that are not yours *Say you're sorry when you hurt somebody *Wash your hands before you eat *Warm cookies and cold milk are good for you *Live a balanced life—learn some, and think some and draw and paint and sing and dance and work some every day *Take a nap in the afternoon *When you go out in the world, watch out for traffic, hold hands, and stick together *Be aware of wonder. Remember the little seed in the Styrofoam cup: the roots go down and the plant grows up and nobody really knows how or why. But we are like that. *Goldfish and hamsters and even the little seed in the white Styrofoam cup—they all die. So do we. *And remember the Dick and Jane books and the first word you ever learned—the biggest word of all—LOOK."

Fulghum continues...

"Everything you need to know is in there somewhere. The Golden Rule and love and basic sanitation. Ecology and politics and equality and sane living.

"Take any one of those items and extrapolate it into sophisticated adult terms and apply it to your family life or your work or your government or your world and it holds true and clear and firm. Think what a better world it would be if we all—the whole world—had cookies and milk at 3:00 in the afternoon and then lay down for a short nap. Or if all governments had as a basic policy to always put things back where they found them and to clean up their own mess.

"And it is still true, no matter how old you are—when you go out in the world, it is best to hold hands and stick together."

Ladies... You Might Want to Just Skip this Part

As a dedicated and proud liberal, I have always prided myself in being a loyal and consistent supporter of equality issues of all kinds.

I was a proud "women's libber" back in the day and can prove it by reciting all the words of Helen Reddy's "I Am Woman." (Hear Me Roar). Note my best version of this is done in the shower, so I am assuming no one will take me up on proving this.

Having said that, I am fully convinced there are still three critical areas holding women back from reaching even greater heights. So... with deep risk, and severe trepidation, and the sure-to-follow incredible regret, I give you these lingering three items.

1. Time spent talking on the phone

2. Time spent in the bathroom

3. Time spent shopping

Sorry, ladies, but it is what it is. Let's quickly analyze the three.

Again, making a huge generalization—call it one giant step for women, one very dangerous step for this writer's mankind—I make the following observations.

1. Women do not know how to close a conversation. They linger at the end, neither party wanting the dreaded end to their beloved vocalization. I am all for social connections and quality conversation, but at a point much quicker for men than for women, it is time to...Wrap It Up! Particularly on the phone. Let's

go. Say good-bye. Things to do. Chores to get accomplished. Note, this applies as well to social parties, where men can get ready to leave in about twenty-five seconds, but women have to make the rounds to say good-bye to everyone they have already talked to for the past three hours. WRAP IT UP. SAY GOOD-BYE. MOVE ON. Your time is valuable.

2. Time spent in the bathroom? Dangerous territory here, I know. Possibly life-threatening if the curling iron has been on long enough. But I speak for many of my male brethren out there in this: We don't know all that you do in the bathroom when getting "ready." Understand that we fully appreciate the preparation and effort you perform to make yourself look as attractive as possible. We also fully appreciate that the process takes longer for women than for men. But and however…somehow, someway you must find a way to make this process quicker. Simply too much time spent in the bathroom. Again, time is valuable. And some of that "bathroom prep" time could be used for more productive purposes.

3. Finally there is shopping. What is it with "shopping"? I can't understand the love here. With most men the goal when visiting a shopping mall is get in and get out as quickly as possible––and that's only if we're forced to go in the first place. (Note: This does not apply to sports memorabilia stores or gadget/electronic stores.)

But women can linger in a store for hours. It is amazing. They savor the shopping experience like fine wine. They buy stuff that they have no problem retuning. Men look at the return line of a local retail store and rate its pleasure level as somewhere above doing taxes and just slightly below being water-boarded. Women? The return line? Not a problem. The return line is just a mere inconvenience, and who knows? While you're at the store…maybe another chance to take another lap around the clothes aisle.

And don't even get me going on the whole shoes and purses thing. I have never understood the fascination with having forty sets of each, matching colors, etc.

But again, all this time women spend shopping—is time spent unproductively. And time is valuable!

So there you have it. My recipe for furthering the women's movement in society.

Less time shopping. Less time talking on phone. And less time in the bathroom.

Time is valuable, ladies. There are things to be accomplished that can't be done in the above three areas. Someone had to say it. I will take the fall for the many silent males out there who I know agree with me.

That is it. Thank you for taking my call, and I will now hang up and listen for your answer. (Which probably will have something to do with the time men spend watching sports while lying on the couch.)

Laugh Trax

Flying is the second greatest thrill known to mankind.
The first is landing.

Every time I look back and reminisce about
how much I miss my youth—
I just think of algebra.

Remember…abstinence should only be practiced in moderation.

I broke my finger today,
But on the other hand, I'm okay.

I never knew what real happiness was until I got married,
but by then it was too late.

If at first you don't succeed…
don't try skydiving.

There is a very fine line between fishing
and standing on the shore looking like a complete idiot.

That is not a beer gut I have.
That is a protective covering for my six-pack abs.

Music Is the Universal Language

never learned how to play a musical instrument in my life. Wish I would have, though. It is something I definitely regret. Sports has always been my first passion.

But more and more, as I get older, music has become a source of great satisfaction.

Very few things in life can fill you with the whole-body "feel good" experience that music can. You want to talk MBHS again? Mind, body, heart, soul? Music can get you right there. It can pull all four of those together—and when it does, it is good. Really good.

A good song can give you that joyful, peaceful feeling that is hard to explain. Almost like taking a good sip of hot coffee or tea or soup on a freezing cold day, and the heat from the warm drink just permeates throughout the body. That kind of "feel good."

Like the Barry Manilow song "I Believe in Music" says, "Music is the universal language and love is the key…to peace, love and understanding and living in harmony."

Okay, maybe that is going a bit too far. And maybe I am one of the few males in my age group willing to admit I used to like (and still like!) the music of Barry Manilow. But in his admittedly sappy way, Manilow was right on.

Music can be bonding. In a special and unique way. No doubt about that.

I treasure the moments I get to listen to music that I really enjoy.

Wise to Surmise

"In the end, we only truly regret the chances that we do not take,
the relationships we were afraid to have,
the decisions we waited to make."
~Maya Angelou

There are not seven wonders of the world in the eyes of a child...
There are seven million.

Dream as if you will live forever.
Live like you will die tomorrow.

The hottest places in hell
are reserved for those who have no opinion.

As you slide down the banister of life
may the splinters never be pointing the wrong way.

The real measure of a person's wealth is how much he would be worth
if he lost all his money.

Jon Cohn

One of the most important trips a person can make
is to meet someone else halfway.

Don't count the days;
make the days count.

Spelling and Grammar...
and Lions and Tigers and Bears—Oh My!

This one has been a lifelong battle for me. And for the most part, a losing one. But the fight marches on...

The battle has centered around my longtime complaint with the overemphasis in school and everyday life (business, reading, emails, etc.) of grammar and spelling. This linguistic conflict has been ongoing since maybe...oh, say kindergarten class with the wonderful and ageless one, Miss Hedges.

Note that I preface this entire diatribe by saying *over*emphasis on grammar—not unimportant or insignificant—just overemphasized. I continue to be amazed how people put grammar and spelling on equal footing—and sometimes even elevated footing—over the content of what one writes.

I had a respected executive friend of mine say that any corporate position job application with a misspelling that comes his way is automatically thrown out. That's right, a potential excellent employee—gone-zo for a spelling error. Into the "also ran" bin, the application goes. I would assume many business execs think the very same way.

Is that really the best judge of business or executive talent or success? Are there other things on that application that might make you later regret your quick hook for the misspell decision?

Did you bother to check and see the experience the applicant has had? Maybe he has done some unique volunteer work outside his field. Maybe he has had an experience in a field where he has really stood out. Maybes he serves on a committee or board outside the field that could bring a unique perspective to the company. Maybe her recommendations from her other endeavors are truly special and glowing. So many potential key items that could impress.

126

But no. A simple misspelling on the application. Sorry, Charlie—or Charlene—you're in the out pile.

Doesn't make any sense to me.

I had numerous English teachers in grade school and junior high and high school who would state with papers turned in, that for each misspelled word there would be one full grade taken off.

I say, *Say what?* A full grade off for a misspelled word? Seriously?

Let me get this straight. A person could write a well-thought-out, well-researched paper with some creative and unique suggestions and ideas. It could be well articulated and well communicated. But with a couple of misspelled words, that individual might get a B- or maybe a C grade—and yet another fine student could write a far less-researched and far less thought-provoking paper—but with perfect grammar, perfect punctuation, and every margin perfectly set--and that person could get a B+?

Do we not have our priorities out of place here?

Again, not that grammar and spelling are not important. But a few misspelled words here and there in a long paper? A colon where a semicolon should have been? A paragraph not properly indented? Please.

In the literary big picture of things…who cares?

What counts as a writer—in my particularly uneducated opinion—is not technically perfect grammar, not a perfectly spelled manuscript, not an aesthetic masterpiece, but rather the writer's thoughts and ideas and connections and creativity and humor and flow and the ability to make it all interesting and thought-provoking, and even emotion touching.

That to me is what good writing is, and that to me is what should be emphasized in school!

I couldn't stand it when my kids were young and learning how to write papers in, say, the third- through eighth-grade years, and seeing the teacher's emphasis on proper grammar and learning proper etiquette and how it subtly stifled, somewhat, the joy and creativity of the young writer's development.

That's right, otherwise excellent and well-trained teachers are following the tradition of making sure grammar is emphasized in young kids' writing, absolutely constricting their creativity. It holds hostage, to some extent, the freedom of thought and the fun of writing.

If I were a grade school teacher in charge of writing—admittedly, a truly scary thought to one and all—I would say, let it flow, children! Let it flow! Let it flow! Let it flow! Write down your thoughts. Write down your ideas! We can work on the handwriting and the grammar and the punctuation later, but write, kids, write!

And hopefully they will find the joy in doing so.

I would concentrate on helping the kids make their writing smooth and understandable. Make their thoughts better connected so people can more easily understand.

The "rules of the road," so to speak, when it comes to punctuation will come in due time. But let those young kids write uninhibited!

Now, if I had to analyze my own writing, I would say it is similar to the way I dress…. I would rather have it feel good than look good.

This grammar topic has long been a pet peeve of mine. And one I have gotten in many arguments over.

Long enough to realize I appear to be in the minority with my thinking, and I clearly understand (notice I did not use the word *respect* here) the fact that many do seem to put such importance on proper grammar.

So I live with it. Sort of. But it hurts.

You know how so much of what we thought when we were rebellious youngsters, always looking for a cause to fight with adults over, now has a completely different perspective? The wisdom of age and experience often renders many of our youthful thoughts and ideas to, at the very least, some hard second-guessing, and at its worst, a complete reversal in thought.

Well, the spelling and grammar issue does *not* fall in that category for me. It is one of the rare instances where I felt strongly about this as a young ten-year-old, and now almost fifty years later...well...I. feel exactly the same way now. Even stronger, actually.

Finally, to wrap this segment up, I want to thank in advance the editors, experts, family members, etc.—whoever it might be as I am typing here—for handling the grammar and spell checking. 'Cause try as I might, I sure as heck wasn't going to catch all the mistakes.... For instance...the spelling of the word *grammar*!!! I always thought it had an *e* near the end (*grammer*), not an *a*. Who woulda thunk it! Certainly not me. God bless spell-check.

Think Twice

I know a guy who was a philosophy major. He couldn't find a job once out of college, but at least he knew why.

Remember: Kids in the backseat can cause accidents. And accidents in the backseat—can cause kids.

Reminder: Never believe in generalizations.

There was the guy who, when dating girls, would not take no for an answer. He did take pepper spray, though, for an answer.

It is indeed lonely at the top. But you do eat better.

A bargain is something you really don't need, at a price you just can't resist.

Be nice to your kids. Remember: They will choose your nursing home.

Cooperation is an eleven letter word
that can be spelled with just two:
W E

The difference between a champ and a chump is *U*

Great Minds Think Alike

There was once a young man who, after working several weeks at his new job, was called in to the human resources office.

"When you applied for this job," said the HR manager, "you said you had a degree in English from Harvard, plus five years' experience in this line of work. Now we find out that you have absolutely no qualifications at all. What do you have to say for yourself?"

"Well," answered the young man, "you said you wanted somebody with imagination!"

Bit and Pieces Magazine
December 2014

Truer Words Have Never...

"The secret to living the life of your dreams
is to start living the life of your dreams today,
in every little way you possibly can."
~Mike Dooley

"Nothing has affected decisions in my life
as much as much as knowing I will die soon."
~Steven Jobs

"What happens to the poorest and weakest among us,
happens to all of us."
~Martin Luther King Jr.

Even if you are on the right track,
you will get run over if you just sit there.

If you want to get even with someone,
do it with someone who did something nice to you.

A hammer does not lose its head,
until it flies off the handle.

Don't go to where the path may lead,
but instead, go to where there is no path, and leave a trail.

"Women who seek to be even with men lack ambition."
~Timothy Leary

The Greatest Job Interview Question Ever

Alright, all you managers and hiring czars out there. Time for some unwanted but nevertheless brilliant business/management advice from your friendly STUFF author. (Who said this book wasn't without some solid meat-and-potatoes information?)

That's right, all you human resource specialists and hiring experts, I give to you now a previously unheard of, but heretofore- soon to be famous question, that when asked in a job interview can best sift out the difference between the ordinary candidate and one that might turn out to be "special." Note: This one, simple question can be applied to any number of work related fields.

As background, this theory of "hiring relativity," originated from an actual argument in a Pony League baseball game—believe it or not. True story.

Okay. Here is the interview question to ask: "Say you were umpiring a baseball game for 13-14 year old boys. It is a playoff game so it is a fairly pressure packed big game. In the final inning the batter with the bases loaded hits a grand slam home run over the fence to win the game.

The crowd is going wild, and the team goes into full celebration mode! But as umpire, you notice the runner, who was on second base to start, while crossing home plate, actually missed touching home plate. Now, after all the runners have crossed the plate—the catcher appeals to you and his coach that he saw the second runner of the four miss touching home plate. The coach comes out to ask for an official appeal.

"Again, to review—you *did* see the runner miss the home plate. The catcher now appeals it to you as the umpire.

"The runner clearly missed the plate. The home run went over the fence. What do you, as the game umpire with the final say, call?"

Here is my managerial theory, if this question is posed to a potential hire in an interview situation…

First of all, based on my vast experience asking this question (remember, this situation actually happened in a real game), about 80 percent of the respondents will answer that if they were umpiring and they saw the runner miss the base, they would have to call the runner out. Most will say they would feel bad about it as an umpire. But you must follow the rules. A rule is a rule, and the kid missed the base. It is a tough lesson to learn—but I would have to call him out, they will say. Adding maybe that if you don't follow the rule here—then why have rules at all?

On the other hand, you will find that roughly 20 percent of the respondents may answer something like this—after some thought. "You know what, I can't call him out. Even though I saw him miss the base, it had zero effect on the play. I can't take this great moment away from that kid and his teammates because of a technicality.

"I know it is against the written rule, but I would have to use my commonsense judgment here…(remember the ball went over the fence. No chance for any play by the defense, so the runner not touching home plate did not have any effect on the actual play). I just cannot call him out on this and take the game away from his team."

Okay, job interviewers and hiring specialists, take notes—here is the key…

If you get anything similar to the latter response—the one that only 10 to 20 percent will give you—the one who says, despite seeing the runner miss the plate, I would still call him safe—HIRE THIS PERSON!! Immediately!

Here is a future employee who will think on his own. Who will not be afraid to go against the "normal way of doing things." An employee who will use judgment and common sense over the "letter of the law." Here is an employee who will come up with different and unique ways to achieve company goals. Here is the employee who will think outside the box. Here is the employee not looking to fit in and just get the job done—but instead who wants to climb the ladder to success and above and beyond.

Worried about the respondent being lax in following rules? Nonsense. When it comes to rules or procedures that truly matter, this employee will likely be there, strong and sure. I have always said that the best employees *and* the best umpires or officials are the ones who don't just know the rules—but much more importantly, know how and when and where to apply those rules.

No rule can cover every situation. Common sense and understanding the spirit of a rule over the letter of the law will always prevail in the end.

Note, we are not saying that the respondent in the 80 to 90 percent can't be a good employee. Of course not. They very well could.

But the likelihood of the one who responds in the minority here becoming a unique and difference-making employee is great.

This theory has most definitely not been tested, nor researched, nor proven in any way, shape, or form, so please be forewarned and enter at your own risk.

But I will stand by it, and put it up against any other single interview question for insight and perspective.

Have you got better ones? Maybe one you have been asked yourself in an interview? We would love to see some examples of unique and different, but very telling interview questions. It could start a good class discussion. Email me at jcsportsandtees@aol.com.

One final note: If the background check on said job candidate reveals severe drug abuse, felony convictions, and/or stealing from previous employers…please disregard the previous 432 words in this book and move on.

If not…then play ball! And hire that would-be umpire immediately.

Keep the Faith

"Everything is all right in the end.
And if it is not alright, then it is not the end."
~Sign seen at Hilda's Place Homeless Shelter

What do these people have in common?

Jennifer Lopez
Steven Jobs
Ben Franklin
L'il Kim
Hilary Swank
David Letterman
Shania Twain
Jim Carrey
Jewel
Tyler Perry
Kelly Clarkson
Halle Berry
Carmen Electra
Kelsey Grammer
Cary Grant

They were all homeless at one time.

Jon Cohn

Shoehorn Revelations

We used to have a segment on our old radio show called "Close Encounters of a Shoe Kind."

My cohost, the "Bigg Dogg," was at the time also working part-time at the Nordstrom shoe store in Chicago and had previously worked at Nike Town, two of Chicago's higher-end shoe palaces.

As salesman at these two locations, he would, more than a few times, get to serve celebrities as customers. Professional athletes would come into Nike Town often with unlimited free expense budgets, and at Nordstrom movie stars, politicians, or any of Chicago's "elite" could walk into the store to buy shoes at any particular moment.

The Bigg Dogg, on the radio show, would describe the different ways he was treated as a salesman.

This, then, became the core of the "Close Encounters of a Shoe Kind" segment: the sometimes-funny, sometimes-maddening, sometimes-heartwarming, and way-too-often sometimes-rude dealings of the celebrity and their shoe-buying encounters with "Dogg" the salesman.

Many of the celebrities Joel would describe were as nice as could be. Appreciative of his work. Pleasantly and effortlessly conversational. Would talk sports with Joel (who was an avid sports fan). Maybe even give an autograph, or better yet, a nice tip at the end.

Others? Joel would be amazed at how they downgraded or just disregarded him as a salesman. Thinking nothing of trying on nine or ten different pairs and then moving on to a different shoe without even picking one out. And worse yet, acting as if conversation with the very affable Bigg Dogg was some sort of personal affront.

Not even bothering with simple courtesies like "thank you," "please," or giving eye contact when being talked to.

How telling that is about the character of these "celebrities."

It goes back to our earlier segment about judging a person by how they treat service personnel. It truly is a window into the character of a person.

This little trickle of information can be used in many areas of life...

So...if you're thinking about someone you are dating and wondering whether this person is really the "right one," take them on a date to buy some shoes. Then watch, observe, and analyze how they interact with the salesperson. Same thing at a restaurant, ticket counter, or any retail store. By the time they finish with the salesman or service employee—you may have your "is he right for the long term?" answer.

In my next book (hold laughter, please), we will have the Bigg Dogg describe his ninety-four "other" uses for the common shoehorn, which he also learned as a shoe salesman. Seventy-two of those, by the way, (just as a tease) are illegal in fifteen of the continental United States.

The Great Potato

Not sure why I even bring this up. I guess it is part of the STUFF in the book.

But I am a huge fan of the potato. Absolutely love "the tater." In any way, shape, or form.

You can hash it, smash it, mash it, grill it, bake it, scallop it, fry it, shoestring it, chip it, even make "tots" out of it—it doesn't matter. I love the potato—unconditionally.

With one exception.

Please do not throw the dreaded "sweet potato" into the "real potato" category. This weird, orangy-looking food item may have "potato" in its name, but it should not—repeat—should not, be included as a member of the real potato family.

The sweet potato clearly arrives under false pretenses. And as for the beauty and elegance of a wonderful Thanksgiving dinner? Nothing can sink it lower than the disturbing look of the orange mush with that marshmallow topping.

You ask me, stuffing or potatoes? It is *"no lo contesto,"* folks. Give me the potatoes every time!

(Stay tuned for equally exciting avocado talk
in the next STUFF book)

Humor Me

Blind girl in bed with guy: "I think your manhood may be the largest
I have ever laid my hands on."
Guy responds: "C'mon…you're just pulling my leg."

Wife says to her husband, "You're always pushing me around and
talking behind my back."
He says, "What do you expect? You're in a wheelchair."

A guy tells his friend he is having sex with
both his girlfriend and her twin.
Friend asks, "How can you tell them apart?"
Guy responds, "Her brother's got a mustache."

The best way to be sure of hitting a target when shooting a gun:
Shoot first, and then call whatever you hit the target.

Give a man a fish, and he will eat for a day.
Teach a man to fish, and he will sit in a boat and drink beer all day.

There are two different theories about arguing with women.
Neither of them works.

An Educational Quantum Leap

Okay, time for a dangerously sharp change of direction in our reading excursion.

Where else but in this fine journalistic excursion will you see "potato talk" followed by—just for kicks—taking on the herculean task of restructuring our entire educational system? A dangerous transition, for sure.

Pause. Deep breath. Exhale. Repeat as necessary.

I am well aware that people have written entire books and dissertations on this subject—but, here for the convenience of our STUFF readers, I, who barely survived four years of undergraduate work to gain my physical education teaching degree, will give you a better and cleaner solution to our educational system's problems—and all in just a few paragraphs!

Think of the time you will save! And no big words, either, so it will be easier to understand.

Okay…here we go. (Note: If you don't typically drink while reading—this might be a good time to start.)

The biggest key in thinking about revising our school system is that you have to wipe the slate clean. By that, I mean you have to completely clear your mind of your previous thoughts and experiences on how "school" works. Let us, for the sake of theorizing, say that we are starting from scratch. Absolute ground zero with no preconceived notions.

Creative education consultant Ken Robinson may have said it best in his TED Conference speech: "What we need in education and schools is not an evolution. What we need is a revolution!"

Let's start at ground zero. I think most of us would agree that in a society, it is a good and positive thing that there is a place (school) where our children can go during the day to be educated by professionally trained adults on items that we deem important for them to know.

A good basic concept.

Okay, so assuming we agree on this, let's embark on an attempt to come up with the best possible way to devise this roughly seven hours we have our kids together in a building.

Remember, we are starting over completely. Total blank canvas. No previous prejudices about what school looks like or what routines or structures we have experienced in the past.

The only thing we are dealing with now is what this "school" should be like. What is the ideal environment? What do we really want them to learn and be introduced to?

Around seven hours per day we have them on location. What should we as adults be teaching the kids during this time period? What should they be learning about? How do we best enculturate them into our society so that we have the best chance of producing solid, positive, happy, and productive contributors to both our current and future world?

So with that as our tipping-off point, I will give you the basic scenario of what I think this "new school" should look like. (Might be a good time now for that first sip of alcohol if you have not already been drawn to do so.) Okay, here we go...

First, the health of our young children is most important. Not just now—but we want them to develop healthy lifestyles. So every day at our "new school," there should be thirty minutes of solid fitness training. It might be running, it might be cycling, or it might be any number of cardio-related and strength-related exercises. But there should be a solid thirty minutes dedicated to keeping the kids in shape, making it fun, and mixing up the routines.

Note, this is not P.E. class. I am not talking about learning soccer, or floor hockey, or basketball, or badminton—or even my personal favorite, dodgeball! If we have time, that can be another class. This slot is for fitness only. Serious cardio time. Working up a good sweat.

In our "new school," kids will be healthier and in better shape.

And they are going to learn and perform better in academics, because when you work out, the blood flows, the endorphins start kicking in, and the brain gets nicely kick-started into full motion.

Next (remember, clean slate here), our "new school" is going to be dedicated to producing well-aware, well-informed, and socially involved students. Ones who are engaged and knowledgeable about what is going on in the world in which they live.

So let's call it Current Events Class. Our kids today are often pain-fully disinterested or badly removed from what is happening worldwide, nationwide, statewide, and even in their very own communities. Despite all the modern technology out there, they have little interest and little knowledge of most things happening, locally or nationally.

This needs to change. And the best thing about this new social awareness emphasis is that kids will thrive in it. If properly taught, it can be a fun, stimulating, thought-provoking class that kids will actu-ally look forward to!

So, in our newly re-created version of school, a major emphasis will be on bringing up children as knowledgeable, questioning young adults who are not only updated on current events but also excited and interested in them. Every day there will be a current events dis-cussion class.

This class will be taught by trained teachers. Strategies could range from just opening the newspaper and discussing key topics at the time, to inviting in guest speakers, to watching a panel discussion on the big screen about a particular topic and then having class discussion time.

Have you ever watched a good panel discussion on TV? One where the guests/hosts are not yelling and talking over each other? The ones where they have intelligent but strongly opinionated experts all weighing in on a topic, but with different perspectives and with different opinions? They discuss/argue the particular topic. All ranges of opinions are expressed.

I don't know about you, but when I watch a program like this I come away from it much better informed. You really learn the different "sides" to the arguments. You better understand the opposition's viewpoint. You better understand the topic as a whole.

Watching a show like this, and following it up with good teacher-led, but student-participated discussion would be riveting! A class that for sure would have energy, education, awareness, and spirited discussion. And along with it, the added benefit of tolerating and maybe even appreciating the value of other people's perspectives and counter-opinions.

Maybe our national education system could sponsor and produce these type of panel-discussion programs to be shown in classrooms.

Either way, a regular, daily current events class would and should be part of the everyday program for our "new school."

Note that one emphasis in our "new school" is on developing not passive, but active learners. Students who are *not* being taught and lectured to, but instead are part of the discussion themselves.

Okay. Two good valuable classes so far. The juices are flowing. The brain blood is moving. Academic adrenaline starts to kick in.

We are just getting started, but already we have better fit students and ones who are aware of what is happening in the world around them.

Next in our "new school" rewrite, we go to the very beginning of the day.

I believe it would make for a very healthy environment within the school if all kids and teachers "huddled" together at the beginning of the day. Not a literal sports huddle, but more like an all-school assembly.

Think sports, where at the beginning of each practice, the coach gathers the team together. Messages are passed on, inspirational thoughts, important reminders, review of the past day, compliments on good things done previously, and constructive criticism on areas that need improvement.

Note the benefit of this being done in a group setting with everyone (students, teachers, and administrators together), thus increasing the sense of a "team."

By bringing everyone together first thing in the morning, our "new school" would hopefully have a much better sense of a "we are all in it together" mentality. Students, teachers, and administrators would all feel a sense of teamwork. The belief here is that with this team mentality as a "background" or foundation, it can only make for a more positive experience for all kids in the school.

There would hopefully be increased support and friendship between the different grades and age groups in the school. Just as on any good sports team, the younger kids would be looking to the older kids for support and guidance, and hopefully the older kids would accept and thrive on the concept of befriending and positively supporting some of the younger kids in the school.

Most grade school auditoriums can handle the whole school. That is where the kids would gather together first thing every morning. High schools or larger schools that cannot fit all students in the auditorium at once could use the gymnasium instead. Anywhere will do, as long as you have all the students together as a captive audience.

The possibilities for these morning "pep talks" are endless. You could have a guest speaker come in. Maybe some student's parent who has done a particularly special thing or has a unique job experience. Maybe someone from any of many charitable organizations could come talk to the kids and inform them about the particular cause they are supporting. It could be the principal bringing up a situation that happened in school previously that may need addressing, like bullying, or a fight, or a discipline situation, and how things could be handled better. It could be mentioning or awarding students who have done something special. It could be students themselves bringing up a situation or a special topic. It could be something that happened in the news the day before. A message from a recently released movie. The death of an ex-graduate of the school. Any kinds of discussions dealing with morals and character and principles and how to best put them into positive action.

There is literally an endless array of potentially valuable topics that could all help the students to think, question, inspire, wonder, analyze, and observe, and just in general get everyone off to a positive and motivated start to the day.

This "first thing in the morning all-school gathering" gets everybody in the proper frame of mind for a solid, energetic, productive day. And again, it almost inherently develops a sense of unity throughout the school.

So...our "new school" is now beginning to take on a vision. A picture with scenery, if you will. And it is looking quite different from our current standard schools—hopefully soon to be of days gone by.

We have introduced a unique and different way to start the day. We have a class for exercise, getting everybody's blood flowing and improving both their physical and mental well-being. And we have a current events/discussion-led class so that are kids are up on what is happening in the world beyond their own lives and their own communities.

Next up on a "new school" restructured program is reading sessions. I am a firm believer in the value of reading. We all know kids today spend too much time on videos and gadgets, etc. No reason to lecture on this topic. We all know it. But what do we do about it?

Easy. Mandatory, regular routine. From first grade through high school. Thirty minutes of quiet reading time. Every day. Not the required reading assigned by a teacher, but instead choose your own.

Bring your own book, magazine, or periodical—whatever it might be—but read. A good, solid quiet "meat and potatoes" half-hour reading time. Every day in school. And follow it up with a fifteen-minute discussion in which kids can bring up different items, and characters, and situations from the books they have been reading.

The post-read discussion could include opinions, questions, funny things, and strange things...whatever. But it basically would be an open-forum discussion of what people have been reading. Get them engaged. Get them to share. The end result (hopefully) is to make reading a standard and enjoyable activity for youth growing up into adulthood, not something they are "required" to do.

Alright, time is now beginning to be a factor. We are using up quite a bit of our seven-hour day, and we haven't even addressed the core academics! Patience, my friends, patience.

Let's see if we can sneak in one more valuable class or session.

If we have time...let's see if we can have a thirty-minute class each day that will teach kids about things they experience in their everyday lives. Actual, real items that they should know, and will benefit from learning, or at least being made aware of.

Let's call this class "Life Skills." (Actually, that is kind of a boring name, but at this writing it's the best I could come up with.)

Here we deal with everything from balancing a checkbook, to washing dishes, to properly checking a receipt, to home safety items, the stock market, nutrition, maintaining a smoke alarm, cashing a check, purchasing light bulbs, the use of basic tools like a hammer and drill, how to change a tire, cleaning a toilet, dusting, figuring statistics for your sports teams.

The potential ideas here could fill a book. But the key is to make it *useful*. And to make it *practical*. Real things that kids can use (and may not currently know) in their everyday lives, both now and into the future.

Moving on...one more thing before we address our core academics.

Some miscellaneous items: Lunchtime? In the "new school" there definitely would be an emphasis on *not* offering junk items as an option. No soft drinks. No sugary sports drinks. No sugar-infused juices. Doughnuts and pastries? Negative.

The kids eat plenty of junk on their own. At our "new school," we aren't going to be fanatical about it—but on the other hand, we are not going to make additional unhealthy foods available.

Kids eat too much junk already! Sorry, but they do. At first, expect some level of uproar, no doubt, from our youthful entities. But once it becomes standard operating procedure, kids will get used to it and come to think of no junk food in the school cafeteria as normal.

How about after-school activities? Music, sports, theater, clubs, etc.? Yes. Yes, yes. And more yes. Add in an exclamation point for good measure!

Extracurriculars are, in my semi-humbled opinion, a huge part of the school and learning experience. These should be strongly encouraged, for sure! I am a firm believer that you learn as much through being part of a club, having a job, or competing in music or sports as you do in science or math class.

So, big-time emphasis on getting all kids (not just the naturally gifted or popular) into some form of after-school involvement.

Now, as we move along, for those feeling like we are slighting traditional academics…you're probably right.

Not that it will make you traditionalists feel any better, but I offer to you one of my favorite learning-related quotes: "Never let school get in the way of your education."

We clearly are placing emphasis in our seven-hour "new school" day in other areas besides science, math, history, etc. But never fear, we do have a plan.

First, to review, we now have a pretty solid and concrete view of how the "new school" day would go.

A morning "team meeting" when messages and life lessons can be passed on to all students. A hard thirty-minute cardio workout every day. A current events discussion class. Quiet reading time. A "life experiences" class, lunch, recess, and after-school activities for all.

So, what have we left out? Oh dear! We clearly have a gaping hole in the teaching of actual academic subjects! What, my goodness gracious, has happened to our beloved math, science, social studies, history, foreign languages, etc.?

Alright, I never said this "new school" idea was perfect. We do have a few kinks to work out. But it can be done.

We do have time left in the day for a couple of these classes each day. Maybe we could switch off, every other day. Have a unit on math and social studies one day. Science and English the next. Most of the basics could still be taught.

I would argue that the majority of students look back on their school days and can point to at least some amount of time spent, in the hard academic subjects, on items they never ended up using.

So in our "new school," we are going to "trim the fat," shall we say. We will teach the academic basics, but lose some of the minutiae that many of us can remember learning but never using.

Additionally, those who want to pursue further a particular subject for an interest or possible future career, can do so in a variety of ways—after-school academic clubs, weekend programs, computer-taught classes, tutors, etc.

Admittedly, we may lose a little bit in our "new school" on the hard-core academics. And if the "testing craze" continues, our students might not score so well. But remember, the tradeoff is that we now have a student body that is motivated, more together in team spirit, up on current events and the world around them, who love to read, and have learned real, practical, everyday skills they can put to use.

Not a bad tradeoff, I would argue.

So, in conclusion, I propose to you a different-looking school day…less formal. More modernized. More practical. More student-engaged. More fun!

Not bad for a barely-made-it-through P.E. major, huh?

Okay, deep breath… We will now get back to our regularly scheduled programming, and if you got this far on this topic, I say to you…
1) Thank you for hanging in there, and 2) If you haven't already, time
now to finish that drink.

Workout Revenge

Maybe it was the extra laps I made him run. It might have been punishment push-ups. A bad grade? Who knows? I certainly can't remember, as it was some twenty-five years ago.

But fitness trainer extraordinaire Adam Smiley finally got his revenge a while back on his old P.E. teacher.

He must have been licking his chops when I signed up and scheduled a one-hour training program with him. I thought it might be fun. Silly me. I wasn't really afraid. I remembered Smiley as a nice, even-tempered, fairly mild-mannered young kid when I had him in class some two and a half decades ago at Pleasant Ridge School in Glenview, Illinois. Even in later years, as I would see him around town, he seemed to be basically that same nice guy.

But that was before our workout session. Once the session started? Different story! Almost like a great athlete who puts his "game face" on and changes personalities once the contest starts. Such was the case with Smiley, who went all Jekyll and Hyde on me. Instantly, he became a raving bundle of high-energy, push-powered, fast-forwarded, semi-maniacal encourager of my forty-five-minute workout.

He gave me a lovely introduction to such wonderful activities as Banana Splits, Russian Twists, Wall Balls, Supermans, TRXs, stomach crunch pedals, and other grisly names not suited for this family-friendly book. Previously I thought these names referred to either strange, demented WWF wrestling moves or maybe some special drink you might order at a fancy bar.

Little did I know they were part of my old grade school student's fitness-infested full-body workout!

To put it mildly, he did not take it easy on his old P.E. teacher. The next morning I was sore in spots I never even knew I had spots!

Smiley had clearly accomplished his goal. He had gotten at least a little bit of revenge against his old teacher. All with a smile on his face, of course.

Oh…and I did learn a few new things from my old student.

He taught his old P.E. teacher about "baby burnout," the interval workout, and most importantly, the value of "locking your butt."

It seemed every torture-filled exercise Smiley recommended involved the importance of locking the butt muscle so as to better isolate the actual muscles you intended to work.

Who knew?

But one thing was quite clear after it was over. It might have taken twenty-five years…but the student had indeed become the teacher.

And his revenge was complete.

My Solution to Bad Golf

Not that I ever played that much, but after many years of really bad golf, somewhere around the age of forty, I finally found the solution to cure the frustration and embarrassment of my bad play.

I stopped playing! Problem solved.

The solution was there all along, and I just never realized it. It was so simple and so easy. Hard to believe I didn't think of it years earlier.

This was the answer I was looking for all along! No more mental fatigue. No more aggravation and frustration. No more embarrassment of looking for a ball on a completely different hole from the one I was playing…and a lot more of a few things, as well. Especially, 1) money, and 2) time.

As every golfer knows, those two can disappear quickly for those with the small-white-ball addiction.

After playing so poorly, though, I decided that if I ever do write a golf book down the road, I may include the following insightful and unique chapters (of which I am, unfortunately, all too familiar with):

Chapter 4: How to correct the slice on your divot

Chapter 7: I took 112 shots. You only took 83. We both paid $95 to play. Now, you tell me who the winner is?

Chapter 11: How to make the swing you just took—where you completely missed the ball—look like a practice swing. (Trust me, folks, this takes practice and technique.)

Chapter 14: How to stay calm when you are lining up your fifth putt

Chapter 17: You know you're in trouble when the first club that needs re-gripping is the ball retriever!

Chapter 20: Throwing your clubs is a great stress reliever (Bonus: Six different techniques of properly sending your clubs airborne)

Final note: I am a nature lover. That's why I play like I do. Remember, the grass in the middle of the fairway is very boring. Short. Well cut. Always the same. But if you like to experience the tall, varying sizes of grass in the rough areas, as well as water, and sand, and trees, and flowers, and rocks, and occasionally a nice barbecue on the lawn of an adjoining yard—then golf with me. I guarantee you will experience "all kinds of nature" in a round of golf with me. And good times will be had by all! (Except maybe by the neighbors, and the foursome in front of and behind us.)

Jon Cohn

Think Tank

"It is amazing how quickly teenagers can learn how to drive a car,
yet remain unable to understand how to work a snow blower,
a vacuum cleaner, or a lawn mower."
~Ben Bergor

"To observe trees is to understand patience.
To observe grass, is to appreciate perseverance."
~Hal Borland

It is easy enough to be pleasant
When life flows along like a song,
But the man worthwhile
Is the one who can smile
When everything else goes dead wrong.

"People usually consider walking on water,
or walking on thin air to be a miracle.
But I think the real miracle is not to
walk on water or thin air,
but to walk here on Earth."
~Thich Nhat Hanhu

Do Not Let Kids Read This!

I am going to go all "adults only" on you with this next comment, so make sure no little kiddies are peering over your shoulder as you read this. For, trust me, they will not be happy with what I am about to say.

I do this with my head down, and propered embarrassment and humblement, but I must state how I feel:

Christmas comes way too often.

Repeat for the reading impaired.

Christmas comes too often. Sorry.

Yes, sorry. But once a year is just too much. I know I am stepping on sacred ground here. I hate to do it, but I gotta go all Grinch-like and tell it like it is.

Now, counselor, if I could, let me explain myself.

First of all, like every kid ever, I used to love Christmas. Some of my best memories as a child were Christmas mornings. Presents. Family. Food. Decorations. You can't beat it! It truly was wonderful. And when you're a kid waiting a year for Christmas to come around… well, it seemed like forever!

So, no problems at all with bad Christmas memories.

But, as many of you are well aware of and have experienced yourself, as you age…time goes a lot faster. I mean, *a lot* faster!

So, for me…and I may be a party of one on this—Christmas and the whole holiday season simply comes too often. It is here far earlier than I am ever ready for it.

Bottom line: I cannot get psyched up and into the proper holiday spirit *every* season anymore. It's too much. Sorry…but such are the facts.

Don't get me wrong. I still love the holiday season. I love the spirit. The sentiment. The warmness. The gatherings of friends and family. The lights—it's all wonderful.

But my point is, it just comes too often, too quickly, to get properly excited about it every single year. Again, this is most true especially as you age. Now, I well understand this is a completely foreign concept and unheard-of thinking to our young crowd out there. But I have to speak for the old fuddy-duddies who experience the calendar turning at way too rapid of a rate.

Despite taking the role of author-Grinch here, I do offer a suggestion. As you know, our little STUFF book is all about solutions—so I temper my complaint with some solid, and very specific suggestions.

Here is my solution. (This is the part when the kids definitely should go to the other room.)

Christmas (Hanukkah, too) should be like the Olympic Games. Celebrate it once every four years.

Perfect solution. Lots of healing time. Lots of time to recharge. Now, when holiday season comes around, you are going to really look forward to it! Imagine the excitement after a long four-year wait. Mom and Dad are going to really be psyched for getting that nice tree and decorating the house. And with the money saved from previous "years off," think of the nice bundle of presents Santa will be able to deliver to the kids.

Think how special the Olympic Games are. Or even the World Cup, if you're a soccer fan. These once-every-four-year phenomena literally reek of excitement and anticipation. We could have this same anticipation-thrill for Christmas and the holidays again! (Instead of, oh boy...here we go again!)

Now I know this is an absolutely horrible idea for anyone, say, under the age of fourteen. The fifteen-to-thirty age group might scale down a bit on this idea, from say horrible to just ridiculous. But c'mon, all you thirty-and-overs? Don't you feel it? Don't you feel like the holiday season is here before you have been able to fully recuperate (spiritually, psychologically, and financially) from the previous year's?

Think of the joy and anticipation as our once-every-four-year Christmas season approaches. Writing and addressing cards, buying gifts, decorating the tree would now be highly anticipated and anxiously awaited occasions!

Hear ye, hear ye! I propose this amendment. Anyone with me? Hello? Anybody out there...

Sounds like crickets as usual. Oh well. You can't blame a man for trying, can you?

Email your thoughts or comments on this topic—as always—to jcsportsandtees@aol.com.

The Rocking Chair Test

heard this a while back, and it really stuck with me. Gave me some great perspective on how to make decisions, both the small ones and even the big ones.

Here is how it goes.

Basically, when you have to make a decision on whether to do something or not, take the Rocking Chair Test. This is how it works: Imagine yourself as old, retired, and sitting back thinking about life. When you are in your rocking chair out on the porch, looking back at your life, how will you view this decision? Will you be happy you chose to do what you did? Or will you regret it?

So next time you have a decision to make, jump ahead in time. Put yourself in the rocking chair, and imagine yourself looking back.

The decisions could be big or small ones. It might be to go the game tonight or attend your kid's third-grade play. It could be whether or not to travel to an old friend's funeral that might be hard to get to. It could be a job decision of staying where you are, or trying another opportunity that has come up. It could be going to a class reunion, or instead playing your regular card game scheduled that evening with your friends whom you so much enjoy. It could be whether you should go into the city to meet relatives who are in town, or stay at home and watch a movie you have rented. Maybe it is whether you should buy expensive tickets to take your kids to a sporting event or a theater production.

The Rocking Chair Test can apply to any number of small and/or larger decisions. There is no right or wrong here. Simply a good way to put the decision into perspective.

Again, when you're sitting back in the rocking chair someday, and you happen to think about this particular choice, how will you feel about the decision you have made?

I thought about this when I read it, and it made sense. More importantly, I started to use it in my everyday life—and it has helped! I started to realize that sometimes the easier, more comfortable decision might not necessarily be the one I should make.

You are never, of course, guaranteed of making the right decision in retrospect. But the Rocking Chair Test might be a good way of thinking about things so you have less regrets later in life.

Jon Cohn

Words to the Wise

Remember, no decision…is a decision.

There is only one place where you start out at the top.
And that is when you are digging a hole.

A chip on the shoulder…indicates wood higher up.

Remember to practice safe lunch.
Always use a condiment.

When all is said and done,
usually more is said than done.

There was the story of the married man who for the past
twenty-five years had spent every night at home.
"Wow, that is really true love," someone said upon hearing that.
No, not really. He is paralyzed.

A day without sunshine
is kinda like night.

Where There's a Will...

Some thoughts from humorist/philosopher Will Rogers:

1. Never kick a cow chip on a hot day.

2. When you're dissatisfied with your life and wish you could go back to your youth...just think of algebra.

3. How did I get "over the hill" without ever reaching the top?

4. Long ago in ancient times, when man cursed and beat the ground with sticks, it was called witchcraft. Today it is called golf.

5. With Congress, every time they make a joke—it's a law. And every time they make a law—it's a joke.

6. The nation is prosperous on the whole. But how much prosperity is there in a hole?

7. Get someone else to blow your horn and the sound will carry twice as far.

8. People are getting smarter these days. Now they are getting lawyers instead of letting their conscience be their guide.

Super Sex

A little old lady was running up and down the halls of a nursing home, lifting up her skirt and yelling "Supersex!"

She passed by an elderly man in a wheelchair, and she did her thing. She flipped up her gown and said to him, "Super sex!"

The older gentleman went silent for a few moments, and then answered, "I'll take the soup."

Song Revisions

The Baby Boomers are, indeed, getting old. Here are some rewrites of famous sixties and seventies tunes to fit more into the current state of our beloved "Boomers."

1. Herman's Hermits: "Mrs. Brown, You've Got a Lovely Walker"
2. The Bee Gees: "How Can You Mend a Broken Hip?"
3. Ringo Starr: "I Get By with a Little Help from Depends"
4. Roberta Flack: "The First Time Ever I Forgot Your Face"
5. Johnny Nash: "I Can't See Clearly Now!"
6. Paul Simon: "50 Ways to Lose Your Liver"
7. Marvin Gaye: "Heard It through the Grape-Nuts"
8. ABBA: "Denture Queen"
9. Tony Orlando: "Knock Three Times on the Ceiling If You Hear Me Fall"
10. Helen Reddy: "I Am Woman, Hear Me Snore"
11. Leslie Gore: "It's My Procedure and I'll Cry If I Want To"

And of course, no list would be complete without:

1. Willie Nelson's famous hit song redone: "On the Commode Again"

(Source: Traditional Witch website)

Best Way to Win an Argument

Want to win an argument? Use this line—and discussion is over. End of conversation.

"I would agree with you. But if I did, then we would both be wrong!"

Don't Let It Rain (Skittles) on My Parade

Just a quick observation on our community parades of late.

Since when did it become the "Candy Caravan"?

It seems every parade now must include a variety of walkers and riders on floats representing different sorts of social and community organizations, all brought together apparently for one common cause: to increase the already overexorbitant amount of sugar and high fructose corn syrup that our kids consume.

Yes, the throwing of candy out onto the streets during the parade has become an almost expected part of any parade now. A while back, it had gotten to the point that my kids would bring large bags to the parade in anticipation of the candy-throwing carnage.

It has made Halloween almost mundane.

But here is the problem. Instead of looking forward to the parade, and the floats, and the bands, and the dancing, and the other delights of the all-American feel-good community parade, they now see this wonderful display as primarily a way to gather and collect large bags of candy.

If you are keeping score at home…this is not good!

Not to mention, the thrill and corresponding danger as hordes of kid race out onto the streets to do battle over the sacred piece of hard rock candy—oblivious to the possibility of being run over by a parade marshal's car or worse yet, the dreaded Shriners' go-carts.

If I were elected mayor of "pick the town of your choice," USA, one of my first decrees would be BRING ON THE PARADES! BUT LEAVE OUT THE CANDY!

Nobody Asked, But...My Movie Awards

My top-five movies of all time:

The Breakfast Club: Besides being clever, funny, and dramatic, it so beautifully depicted how silly cliques in school actually are, and that the only thing that separates us from being friendly and respecting each other is just getting to know each other! (Bonus...huge early years' crush on Molly Ringwald.)

The original *The Poseidon Adventure*: Still one of my all-time favorites. The best of the "disaster movies." Phenomenal cast. Memorable scenes, such as the "tidal wave" approaching and Shelley Winters swimming underwater. (Note: These two were unrelated.)

Dog Day Afternoon: Al Pacino's breakout movie. Great story. Great emotion. High-level intensity. Surprises along the way. Vastly underrated movie.

Love Actually: A "chick flick"? Maybe. But I loved it. Heartwarming. Touching. Humor. Pathos. Great cast. Can watch it multiple times...and still enjoy. Somehow, someway, this seemingly innocent movie really dug deep.

Airplane: Still the best comedy of all time. Spoofs literally everything. Relentlessly. Makes fun of all the disaster films. Leslie Nielson makes a huge leap through from serious actor to comedy, as does Lloyd Bridges. "Shirley, you can't be serious." "Yes…I am serious…and don't call me Shirley."

My favorite movie scenes of all time:

1. The group celebration in their dad's TV and appliance store after hearing their potential hit song played on the radio, in the movie *That Thing You Do!* It is not a critically acclaimed or even "important" scene. But for pure feel-good…one of my all-time favorites.

2. Gene Hackman as a preacher, giving a Sunday-morning sermon on the cruise ship in *The Poseidon Adventure.* The scene in the very beginning of the film. To me one of the most memorable lines of any movie I have ever seen. After preaching a sermon about "living life the best that you can, being good and moral, and working a good, hard earnest day's work," he concludes, "do not pray to God to solve your problems. But live life the best that you can, be the best person you can be…and then God will pray for you." Solid gold advice. Delivered perfectly by a young Gene Hackman. This became a foundation for my religious philosophy. You want to talk the equivalent of a good cut of steak as an actor in the movie world? Gene Hackman. All T-bone and rib eye and throw in a nice baked potato just for kicks.

3. Al Pacino's "Attica! Attica! Attica! Attica!" scene from *Dog Day Afternoon.* Raw. Can't think of a better way to describe it. Just peeled-away layers of pure, solid

"raw drama." Pacino at his best (which says a lot!),
igniting a crowd as he desperately seeks to avoid capture. From what I heard, the scene was actually not
planned. It just started with one Attica reference and
then, getting lost in the moment and his character,
Pacino went all volcanic—verbal hot lava just started
spewing—with the street-watching crowd egging
him on. And the rest is history.

Again sticking with the theme of movies, and the theme of nobody
asked me but...I give to you:
The two most underrated acting jobs of all time. (They got
acclaimed and nominated—but they should have won outright
Academy Awards.)

Don Cheadle in *Hotel Rwanda*: He got his dues for
this...but not enough. A simply riveting performance,
beautifully portraying the attempt to stay calm and
cool as a respected hotel owner under some of the
most horrific conditions of the Rwanda massacres.
Brilliant acting. And Cheadle is on screen in just
about every scene.

Will Smith in *The Pursuit of Happiness*. With his first
real step into serious acting, the Fresh Prince put on
a performance for the ages. Everything good acting
should be, Smith displayed in this film. All the ranges
of emotion and not too overplayed. He got accolades
for his performance here—but to me it was one of the
best single acting jobs in any movie. Should have won
gold (or an Oscar).

Saddest movie scene of all-time:

> With all the dramatic and heart-wrenching moments
> that have been so well depicted over the years in
> varying movies, this scene certainly does not rank
> up there in "significance." But if you talk sheer sad-
> ness of the moment and the way it was captured (and
> acted), the one that got to me was Emma Thompson
> in the scene from *Love Actually*, where she opens her
> Christmas present from her husband and it is a music
> CD, not the nice jewelry she secretly saw her hus-
> band buying. Immediately upon opening, she realizes
> her husband's suspected affair with his secretary is
> for real, but it is Christmas and her kids are in mid-
> Christmas bliss, so she must hide the disappointment
> while being internally crushed. She rushes into the
> bedroom for a brief moment. It is a strong, powerful
> moment for sure. Perfectly displayed by the brilliance
> of Emma Thompson. Above all, you just really felt her
> sadness. It is a direct hit to the viewer—and it digs
> deep into the gut.

Stop and Smell the Roses... and the Violets, and the Sounds of the Willow Tree, and...

F unny how little things can stay with you…

I had a college teacher once take us outside on a particularly nice spring day. I don't remember what class it was for. I don't even remember the teacher's name. But I do remember a comment he made and his lesson for that particular day.

He said, "We typically depend on one of our senses way too much. Seeing and our eyesight is the dominant sense. Sometimes at the expense of the others."

He asked us to complete a very simple exercise of closing our eyes and just listening to what sounds we could hear. He did the same with closing our eyes and seeing what aromas we could pick up. Repeat for the sense of touch.

It wasn't a breakthrough moment. It wasn't some piece of brilliant philosophical, professorial teaching. Just some simple advice that I took to heart. And every once in a while I will stop myself and try to remember that lesson. It works. Sounds and smells and tactile experiences are so simple and yet so often underappreciated (if appreciated at all!). He was right. We rely our eyes too much. It is wonderful to just stop and concentrate on the sounds all around us and really soak them up. Same with smell and taste.

The older you get…the more the lesson applies. The simple things in life truly are some of the most beautiful—if you let them be.

A little "schmaltzy," I admit. But true.

Wayne...Something?

While we're on the topic…

I remember another small lesson that always stuck with me, again from a teacher whose last name I cannot remember. But I know his first name was Wayne. He may have written a few books. He was an "expert" of some renown. But no chance in heck I can remember his last name, so we will just call him Wayne Something.

The class that Wayne Something taught was for a continuing ed class during my teaching years, and to be honest, as I vaguely remember, the class wasn't all that great. Wayne Something was a nice guy, but not a great, exciting teacher by any stretch.

But, strangely, I do remember one thing he said during one particular class.

He said, you have to enjoy some moments in life without being so verbal. We all love to talk, he said, but there are some times when we should savor certain moments and not let the verbal dominate.

I remember he used the example of a restaurant. "If it is a cheap, fast-food restaurant, where the food is nothing special, then talking and verbalizing is fine, but," he said, "if you are at a really nice restaurant, and eating a particularly special and expensive meal, then concentrate on the food. And the taste"—not so much on talking.

Interesting. I found some truth in this. You see people at these nice restaurants and they are often gabbing away while eating. Now, we all like a little dinner conversation, and talking during a meal becomes a habit of sorts, but the meal is costing you big bucks! More importantly, that lobster, or that veal, or that steak you are eating has a taste you don't get to savor very often.

So, slow down. Ease up on the conversation and concentrate on the sense of taste. Really get into the experience of eating.

That, of course, was just one example. And I do see this as I observe everyday experiences, the almost nervous, incessant need to verbalize. Quiet and silence can be golden, if only for a few seconds.

Deep breath. Relax. Don't be afraid of quiet moments, or pauses in the conversation. Let the game come to you—so to speak.

I think Wayne Something's message was to savor the moments that are special. And don't verbalize those moments away, thus taking away your full appreciation of them.

Wayne Something—wherever you are…and I do hope you still "are" in the present tense—thank you for that little piece of advice that has always stayed with me.

The Affliction of Loss

As we age, there are a number of different health issues that we can be afflicted with. Many of them serious in nature ranging from diabetes, to cancer, to Alzheimer's, and all points in between.

I have always said, if you have your health, all other problems in life are a distant second. Health is, indeed, everything.

But even for those who have not contracted any serious health problems, as you age, problems of a more minor nature can occur.

I call it the "affliction of loss." Nothing serious. Just a little "loss" of many things. But it takes its toll.

We lose our hair (my hand is raised), we lose our hearing (my hand up again), our vision gets worse (my hand was up on this about fifty years ago), we lose our memory (yep, hand up again), we lose our physical conditioning and our muscle tone (I'm hanging on here), we lose our ability to stay up late (me again), and we lose the use of a variety of unspoken things mostly dealing with the urinary tract and thereabouts (no comment here).

The "affliction of loss" rarely strikes quickly. It usually sneaks up on you gradually. Very, very gradually. Usually you don't even notice it—that is, until you start looking in the mirror more carefully and/or your spouse not so gently reminds you for, say, the fifteenth time.

But again, nothing major here, and if you can keep your sense of humor while you are losing many other things, you will get by just fine.

But never take good health for granted. As the old expression goes, "Health is wealth."

A Slippery (If Not Dangerous) Slope

Danger lurks at any moment.

Crowds gather in large numbers, excited yet nervous. Speed and strength are often required—just to get your turn! Agility and athleticism and awareness are often key ingredients for success. And when you are done, your job is not over. Still more danger awaits.

What activity are we talking about?

Not hockey, or auto racing, or any particular dangerous Olympic event.

Instead I bring to you in all its full regalia, the tired, the brave, the strong, the many—who pride themselves in using public sledding hills on a crowded day during the winter months.

True warriors these brave folks are.

If you haven't had young children, or a sudden urge yourself to live out a snowy fantasy from days gone by, you may not be aware of the "every man for himself" maniacal mentality that goes on in these winter wastelands. These public sledding hills, are often packed, crowded, and unsupervised. It is Darwinism at its finest. Survival of the fittest in the battle to get to take your turn. The rules and regulations sign that is posted? If it is still standing, it certainly is rarely noticed. It is obeyed about as much the rookie substitute teacher in a junior high social studies class. Maybe worse.

But there is something about that public sledding hill. Old school fun. Still worth the trip, for sure.

Yes, sledding. Good old, honest-to-goodness fun. Pure. Unadulterated. Unsupervised. Great exercise. Fresh air. The benefits are limitless.

It is, thankfully, a way for kids and adults to get away from the computer, the video games, the iPhones, etc., during the dreaded winter months, and get outside for some good old-fashioned recreation.

But don't kid yourself. These sledding hills are not for the faint of heart. Once you climb to the top of the stairs on a busy snowy day, it is buyer-beware and every man/woman/child for themselves.

There are no referees. There are no officials. There is no supervision. In a sense, that is part of the beauty of it.

In the over-programmed, over-organized society that we have built for our kids, it is nice that the sledding hills provide a little bit of a recreational reprieve from all this.

But be forewarned. And ride downhill at your own risk.

Yes, on a busy, crowded day at the sledding hills, you will witness many near-collisions and more than likely some actual ones.

Just for kicks, let's briefly paint the picture of the sledding hill experience.

First comes the climb up the stairs. This alone can be a bit of a battle, as tired legs, large sleds, and narrow stairs can cause some tension-packed congestion. But we're just getting started.

Once you reach the top, it is the battle for takeoff position. This can be an interesting exercise unto itself. There are a lot of people at the top, and not all that much room. Remember, no supervision, no rules. Just kind of jostling for position, and it becomes the mountaintop version of "survival of the fittest."

If you are lucky enough to get in position for the downhill takeoff, then the real fun begins. Heading down the hill with a great amount of speed and dodging all the other sleds without incurring any full-speed head-on collisions and/or tipping over.

If you do manage to make it down the crowded freeway of snow-dressed patrons and sleds without damage or collision, temper your joy and excitement—for ladies and gentlemen, your job is not yet done. Veteran sled enthusiasts know that at the bottom of the hill… danger lurks yet again.

Yes, just as you finish your ride and wait at the bottom of the hill, momentarily catching your breath, you get the added thrill of looking up and watching speeding sled-shaped missiles headed your way. Beware. And don't delay! Get your sled, pick up your young children, and move quickly!

Remember the old saying of the veteran sledsters: "Those who stay in vain, will feel the pain."

So, bottom line, folks, enjoy all the beauty and fun of your local public sledding hill, but by all means, remember to sled responsibly—and do watch out for the other guy!

Bumper Sticker Keepers

Some goodies from the backs of a few cars, trucks,
and other assorted vehicles...

KEEP HONKING...I'M RELOADING

THE SHORTEST SENTENCE IS "I AM"...THE LONGEST IS "I DO"

DRIVER CARRIES NO CASH. HE'S MARRIED.

FOUR OUT OF THREE PEOPLE HAVE TROUBLE WITH FRACTIONS

DRUGS LEAD NOWHERE...BUT IT IS THE SCENIC ROUTE

I TRIED TO CHILD-PROOF MY HOUSE...BUT THEY STILL GOT IN

MAKE LOVE, NOT WAR?
DO BOTH—
GET MARRIED!

A Bishop, a Nun, and a Donkey

An aspiring young journalist was helping to write for his local church newsletter. Things did not go so well…

One time, the pastor of the church entered a donkey into a local community donkey race. The donkey ended up winning the race, but the headline he wrote in the newsletter read, "Pastor's ass ends out in front!"

The bishop of the church was, of course, not happy with this, so he told the pastor he must break from tradition and remove the champion donkey from the regional competition. But the overanxious journalist slipped up again. Next week's newsletter headline? "Bishop scratches pastor's ass."

The pastor had had enough. He then gave the donkey to the nuns in the nearby convent. The headline for that week? You guessed it. The young scribe wrote, "Nun gets best ass in town."

When the bishop read this, he practically fainted. He told the nun to sell the donkey immediately. She found a local townsmen who bought the donkey for twenty-five dollars. Our little troubled journalist's headline for the following week? "Nun sells ass for twenty-five dollars."

The bishop was now furious. He buys back the donkey himself, takes it out to an open prairie, and let the donkey go.

He thinks, finally, the nightmare headlines are over.

Next week, the feature story for the newsletter is titled, "Nun announces her ass is finally wild and free."

…the young scribe is now selling real estate in another part of the country.

(Source: Jokegarden)

Morning Pick-Me-Up: Caffeine and...the Obituaries

Along with brushing my teeth, washing my face, visiting the commode, and making coffee every morning, I have welcomed a new member to my "morning routine team." That's right, sneaking in right between the almighty cup of caffeine pick-me-up and the always life-enhancing morning shower, I have become an avid and daily reader of the newspaper obituaries.

Hey, you never know where inspiration can come from.

Now, they say man is a "routine-oriented species." I think that might be connected with Maslow's hierarchy of needs pyramid. But maybe not. Maslow was a complicated guy. As a side note to Mr. Maslow (does anyone actually know his first name?), I don't know where he put going to high school basketball games to kill the dredge and boredom of long, cold Chicago winters, but for me that is somewhere on the very base foundation of my personal hierarchy of needs. It may come after food and water, but clearly before human communication and sleep.

If Maslow saw me in the morning? Well, proof-positive that man is routine-oriented. I've got it down to a science. The regimen is quite strict.

Especially with the morning paper. Order is key here.

I always go to the front page first, then to the arts section, then to the business section, and then to the obits, before saving the best for last...the sports page! Which, here in Chicago, and being a lifelong Cubs fan, very nicely fits right after the obituary section.

But, getting back to the point of this little section, I have found reading the obituaries to be all things, including uplifting, inspirational, sad, tragic, funny, informational, and thought-provoking.

1. There are items that stick with me from reading these end-of-life passages. I see the ages of the people who have passed away and the various group of fifty-somethings, sixty-somethings, seventy-somethings, and eighty-somethings that inspire me and remind me that if I have been thinking about doing or accomplishing something, I'd better do it! Time is a'wasting, as they say. Reading the ages of those who have passed away becomes a not-so-gentle reminder to get off your hesitation cloud, and if you're thinking about doing something—do it! Life is short.

The old expression, "Live each day as if it were your last, for one day you will be correct," applies beautifully here!

2. I look for names that I may recognize. Old friends, neighbors, schoolmates, parents' friends, maybe a relative on non-speaking terms, work and play contacts over the years. At my age, if you peruse long enough, you are bound to come across some names from days gone by. Typically, I will see a couple of names per week that I recognize or remember.

3. It is fascinating reading about the lives of these people. Obviously it's very sad they have passed away. But it's also uplifting to read the wonderful tributes and great memories that family members have posted. You may not know them. But their stories can inspire.

4. The final reason I find the obits an uplifting morning read? I'm not in there! Always a good thing. And as a side note, it does make you wonder, when it is your

time, what will be written about you? Writing your
own obituary is definitely not cool...but you can
drop some subtle hints to loved ones about items you
may want to appear—or maybe more importantly—
not appear.

The MOPED Religion

I never really bought in to the motto of "If you can't beat 'em, join 'em." Instead, I tend to go by the opposite, that being if you can't join 'em, beat 'em.

This kind of applied to how I developed my views on formal religion as I aged over the years. And certainly the term "beat 'em" would not apply to religion at all. Obviously there is no right or wrong here, and for everyone it is a personal decision and belief set.

As for myself, I never really connected with the rituals and historical beliefs of various traditional religions. So...I started my own!

Again, formal religious practice just never hammered home with me. Never really got down to my gut—which if religion is as it should be, is exactly how you should feel about your particular faith.

Having said that, I very much enjoy going to church. I married into a Catholic family, and we on occasion—but not regularly—do attend services. I enjoy going. I enjoy the quiet. The peacefulness. The music. And although I don't follow the formalities—for me, I don't kneel and pray or take communion—I do stand at the appropriate times and enjoy the time for pensive thought.

The fact that my younger son and myself have developed a tradition over the years always ending out in a feigned pushing/shoving match after the "peace be with yous" should not be seen as a sign of disrespect. Just a little friendly family tradition.

But here is the key...although I don't follow a particular religion or any of the formal "traditions," I do consider myself "spiritual."

I think about, and ponder, and wonder, and question all the time the existence of the beyond. What is life all about? What happens after we physically die? Is life strictly biological? How did we get here? And the thousands of other questions just about everybody asks.

So...

Somewhere, in my teens, and most importantly *before* the moped motor vehicle was ever invented (man, did that take the steam out of my created name), I came up with my own name for my particular religion, and called it MOPED.

MOPED...My Own Practiced Every Day

In the MOPED "religion," it is basically about being a good, and moral, and caring person 24/7. Each and every day. Nothing too dramatic here.

We don't look above for help. We don't ask for forgiveness on Sundays. We don't follow any particular rituals. We simply believe in living life in the best possible moral way.

The MOPED religion believes there must somehow, some way be more to life than just strict evolution and biology. There are too many amazing things in this world, from nature, to space, to the complexities inside the human body, for it all to be strictly biological and solely from evolution. There has to be something else to it, doesn't there?

Lying on a blanket outside, on a clear night, in, say, Michigan and looking up at the incredible vastness of the sky and the wondrousness of the stars should convince us of this. Or sitting on a beach and looking out at the never-ending horizon of the water.

You feel the expanse of nature. Of the world. Of the universe.

Here is what MOPEDS believe.

We simply don't know what is beyond us. We are probably not meant to. What it actually is, is probably so far beyond our comprehension that not only can we not speak of it—we probably can't even think of it. Let alone write it down on paper.

But there must be something else, right? Something? To explain the vast beyond that we can and cannot see?

I guess all we can do is wonder. But it is actually kind of cool, and strangely comforting, to think about it all.

So the MOPED religion (again standing for My Own Practiced

Every Day) signals to each person to live their life the best they can. To find ways to be happy and, more importantly, to find ways to help others be happy, as well. All the good and moral teachings many religions profess, but without any of the more formal "trappings."

Heaven and hell, and God, and Jesus, and the Bible, and all other traditional religious beliefs may just be a part of human nature to put something finite into the vast unknown.

We are not sure of all of the above. But we are sure of the value of charitable work, helping others, and assisting those in need any chance you get.

Our theory is, "The slightest bit of good is better than all the best words and intentions," and additionally we live by the non-religious creed of "Don't pray to God to solve your problems. Instead, live life the best you can…work hard, and be honest and moral, and whatever it is that is beyond us…will then pray for you."

It is, indeed, a simple concept, developed circa somewhere in the late sixties. A dangerous time to develop anything, really, let alone a new religion. But this is what I came up, and how exactly is kind of a foggy memory. (Not unusual to teenagers in the late sixties, by the way.)

Membership in our group is extremely available. So far the MOPED religion has basically one member. Me. Not exactly a riveting following.

But new members are welcome anytime! No sign-up necessary. No fees involved. And the initiation is no more painful than buying me a beer or a cup of coffee.

As always, if you do have thoughts or ideas regarding this concept, by all means we are happy to start a discussion. The email address again is jcsportsandtees@aol.com.

Note: Sorry, no "MOPED" mugs or T-shirts on sale at this site. But, again, the sign-up fee is beyond reasonable.

The Smiles-High Club

A mother and her five-year-old son were flying Southwest Airlines from Kansas City to Chicago.

The son, who had been looking out the window, turned to his mother and asked, "If big dogs have baby dogs, and big cats have baby cats, why don't big planes have baby planes?"

The mother couldn't think of an answer for that one, so she told her son to go ask the flight attendant.

The boy then got out of his seat, walked down the aisle into the flight attendant galley, and asked the flight attendant, "If big dogs have baby dogs, and big cats have baby cats, why don't big planes have baby planes?"

The flight attendant said, "Did your mother tell you to ask me?"

The boy said, "Yes."

"Well, then," said the flight attendant. "Tell your mother there are no baby planes because Southwest Airlines always pulls out on time. Have your mom explain that to you."

Jon Cohn

Thinkers and Stinkers

Some things simply make you wonder—if you stop to think about them...

1. If a vacuum "sucks," is that good or bad?

2. Why do having a "fat chance" and a "slim chance" mean the same thing?

3. Why do we sing "Take Me Out to the Ball Game" when we are already at the game?

4. Have you ever noticed that the word *phonics* is not spelled like it sounds?

5. Why are sports-stadium structures called "stands" when they are really for seating?

6. If all the world is a stage, where does the audience sit?

7. If love is blind, why do they make lingerie?

8. How come *abbreviated* is such a long word?

And finally...

1. Why doesn't glue stick to the inside of the bottle? (This one has stayed with me for way too long.)

Good Food...for Thought

"When you have completed 95 percent of your journey—
you are but halfway there."
~Japanese Proverb

"I am not an environmentalist…
I am an Earth warrior."
~Daniel Cherry

"Ambition can take you very far—
but when you get there, who are you?"
~Garrison Keillor

"Don't go to where the puck is—
go to where it is going to be."
~Hockey great Wayne Gretzky

Three keys to successful public speaking:
Be to the point, be brief, and be seated.

"If the meek are going to inherit the earth,
then our players are going to be land barons."
~Football coach Bill Muir

"We make a living by what we get,
but we make a life by what we give."
~Winston Churchill

Great Ideas Are Hiding Everywhere

Iam convinced from observation, it is not that hard to be a success. It doesn't take any particular level of creative brilliance. And it certainly doesn't take an advanced degree in higher learning for any individual out there to come up with ideas and inventions that can 1) make a real difference in the world, and 2) make them lots of money!

The simplest of good and useful ideas are out there every day right before our eyes. All we need is to keep those eyes open and let them wander a bit in conjunction with the creative cortex part of our brain.

That's right, just by observing the things around us, and maybe adding in a slight dash of good old out-of-the-box thinking, you, too, could stumble upon the "next great thing." Really. Great ideas are sitting out there just waiting to be plucked, all with surprisingly simple solutions. We just need to think about them a bit.

Examples? Glad you asked.

I will give you a classic one. Not a dramatic, or life-altering one— but simply an example of how good moneymaking ideas are right out there for us—just waiting to be discovered.

Let's talk vending machines (for candy, snacks, soft drinks, or whatever) for just a brief moment. For many, many, many years, the standard-dose vending machines would have a slot for change only. The product would be for sale for 50 cents or 25 cents or 75 cents, but you could only get the product if you actually had change on you. They did not have dollar bill–slot capability.

Back in the day, this was just accepted. No one thought much about it. If you didn't have change, you were out of luck. No snacks for you, mister. But really, no big deal. That's just the way it was in the wonderful world of vending machines.

Then, *presto!* Someone came up with the idea of putting a dollar bill slot in the machine itself that could dispense change. Nothing overly brilliant here. It is commonplace on almost all vending machines now. Looking back at it, it was a pretty simple and reasonable concept.

Now, here is the key. I am sure this technology was easily available all along—not exactly rocket sciencetry here, I wouldn't think. But because of this small but brilliant idea, all of a sudden all the people who could not purchase product—and remember, vending machines usually are for spur-of-the-moment purchases—could now use the dollar bill slot and more easily increase their ability to raise their cholesterol levels and sodium content—all this, and still get change back!

I don't know how much this increased vending machine sales. But I would be willing to bet maybe as much as 30 percent—a huge improvement.

Not exactly an invention that made a social difference in society... but whoever came up with the idea surely made a lot of money for both their company and hopefully themselves.

But the crucial point here is that the technology was already there. Anyone could have come up with this concept. It was just an idea somebody had to look at and think about.

As stated in the beginning of this section, it does not have to take creative genius or academic brilliance to come up with good, solid inventive ideas. Instead, just a keen observation of everyday life and how things maybe could be improved. Sprinkle in a little curiosity. Add a dash of outside-of-the-box thinking, and *boom! Presto!* There you have it. Good ideas. New inventions. Maybe some monetary rewards—call it a "finder's fee" for the one who thought of the idea.

Want a second example?

How about the "seconds until light changes" markings now displayed on traffic signals in most cities at busy street intersections?

When they first came out, I was a bit skeptical—in fact, I looked at them as maybe an added nuisance.

But I think most of us now would agree that once you get used to them, these crosswalk timing devices are very helpful! If you are a walker in these crowded street areas, I think you have come to appreciate the seconds-until-light-changes countdowns. It makes walking across the busy intersections in the city just a little less like a near-death experience and brings it down to maybe a nice, simple cautionary challenge (but don't kid yourself—still life-threatening if you aren't "on your game" and paying attention).

Now, again, here is an idea that could have been installed many, many, many years ago. The technology is quite simple, and it could have certainly been implemented decades ago.

But someone, somewhere, came up with the idea to put the seconds-till-light-changes warnings on the traffic signals. Simple, easy to install, and most importantly, very helpful! The brilliance is in the simplicity!

As a special reader bonus (yippee!), I am going to throw out two examples of my own that I have been thinking about for a while. Neither of these have been invented yet. Both are simple to produce.

I am basically too busy writing a book to take time to figure out how to manufacture, patent, and market the products. So I will throw them out to the first interested reader who wants to roll with them.

If successful, a simple 10 percent "finder's fee" would be all that is asked. If unsuccessful, you have my contact info, and you know where to find me.

Have your people talk to my people, and we'll do lunch…

Here are my two ideas.

Bathroom Breakthrough and Head-Butt Protectors

For my first win-vention, I introduce you to the "Swipe after Wipe." A simple concept, really. But to explain its need, we do have to get a bit graphic in a slightly touchy area. So let's give it a try.

Alright...so...here we go. Saying this win-vention will revolutionize bathroom use from coast to coast might be going a bit far. But the product is long overdue. See if you agree. Here's the plan. After sitting down on the toilet, we all use toilet paper for "cleansing" our rear ends, usually done with a few not-so-gentle wipes. All of us afterward then go to the sink to wash our hands with soap. Normal standard operating procedure. No problems here, except...this: Between the wiping (sorry, if you're eating while reading this) and the sink, there are multiple steps where the germs—or worse—can be spread.

Let us count thy ways. First you have to stand up and pull up your pants. Germs on your pants right off the bat. Second, depending on the pants, you may have to buckle the belt. Now we have germs on the belt buckle, as well. Third, you have to flush the toilet using the handle, and fourth, you have to touch the sink handles to turn on the water. All this is done *before* applying any disinfectant soap.

So...if you think about it—and I admit, it is best *not* to think about it—germs (or worse, if you are not a good wiper—think young kids here!) are now potentially spread to multiple areas.

This, my friends, is a problem. One that has never, as far as I know, been addressed. Until now. So, to you, the semi-dedicated STUFF reader (at this point, you are probably questioning any dedication at all to this book, but stay with me here...), we offer you real, concrete answers and solutions to all the problems that plague society—including those of the bathroom variety.

We have described the problem.

The solution? Simple. Has anyone ever even thought of putting soap disinfectant—the kind you wipe on your hand without having to rinse—right in the tube handle of the toilet paper dispenser? That way the disinfectant is right there for you before you touch anything else! How hard could that be to do?

It could involve a dispenser opening on the end of the roll, in the middle, or anywhere you could push and get your splash of disinfectant soap. Easy to design, no doubt.

Problem solved, right? Brilliant in its simplicity? Technology for this, I would think, would be about as basic as it could be. And better yet, no maintenance required! Just refill the soap as needed. A couple of "swishes" from the tube dispenser, and your hands are at least mostly disinfected *before* you have touched your pants, the buttons, the belt, the sink, the flush handle, etc.

Brilliant! Absolutely brilliant! Thank you.

My second win-vention is to be called the "Heading Band."

Very simple. For soccer players only. Have you seen this game played in recent years? It is becoming more and more of a physical game. Watch from the World Cup all the way down to the youth leagues, and you will see head collisions on a regular basis—even some of the more violent variety.

The collisions happen in a number of ways out "on the pitch." The most violent and concussion-threatening come from the head butt, when two players jump up to try to head an up-in-the-air ball—and heads collide fighting for the air ball.

But there are numerous other instances in soccer when head collision can occur. Using the head to deflect or direct kicked balls is one, as well as occasionally an opposing player getting the foot too high in attempt to get the ball and making contact with a player's head. Often a player can fall to the ground hitting their head, or worse yet, while on the ground in a scrum situation, get accidently kicked in the head.

In any or all of those scenarios, the contact to the head may be significant. The possibility for concussion ever-present. More and more the public awareness over concussions, and their long-term effects, has become a factor with kids and parents and players all participating in this great game. The science is out there. The studies have been well documented.

Yet, having said all this...

NO PLAYERS IN SOCCER WEAR ANY HEAD PROTECTION! With all the talk and the studies on concussions? With all the collisions soccer has involving the head? And still no protective equipment for the heads of the players?

Hard to believe. Really. But as usual, your friendly STUFF author comes riding to the rescue!

Again, an amazingly simple solution is right there for you—for all soccer players. Make it a requirement to wear a protective headband. Just like in football with the helmet. Make it specifically for soccer. A headband, not a helmet. But it should be well-padded and wider— much more so than the standard, say, tennis terry-cloth headband.

The "Heading Band" is long overdue. This could be a huge money-maker for any industrious soul. It could be made in a variety of lovely attractive colors. It could be part of the uniform and even a fashion statement of sorts. You could even put team logos on there, or maybe some message meant to intimidate the opponent. But whatever it looks like, it would be wide enough and padded enough to protect the brain area from repeated collisions and significantly improve the future health and mind power of our soccer athletes playing today—both young and old.

I really can't believe they don't have a product like this already. And if they do, I can't believe players aren't required to wear them.

Thinking I am being too soft here? Think I am being overly dramatic? Just think about the sport of hockey and goalies back in the forties, fifties, and early sixties. They never wore masks. None of any kind. Nothing to protect the face.

When goalie masks first came out, everyone laughed at them. They thought goalies (where have you gone, Jacques Plante, Glenn Hall, Eddie Giacomen?) were being wimps for wearing any kind of face protection.

Now, of course, *every* hockey goalie in the world wears a mask.

You suggest today to a hockey goalie—at any level—to play without a mask, you would be laughed at immediately before being handed a summons for a lawsuit. The "Heading Band" will follow the same path for soccer players.

So there you have it. Two amazingly simple inventions. Guaranteed to be winners.

But the bigger picture is this: Remember, there are many more simple and winning examples waiting to be discovered out there in our everyday lives. All we have to do is keep our eyes open, observe, and think a little bit, and the possibilities are endless.

If anyone wants to work with me on the two win-ventions mentioned above…you know where to get a hold of me (jcsportsandtees@ aol.com).

If you decide to take the idea and run with it on your own, be careful. I have good lawyers and a sort-of friend named Guido who "knows people."

But if you want to work with me on this…God bless you, and best of luck. And don't forget my 10 percent!

Jon Cohn

Sidewalk Sharing

Not breaking into any critical social dramatic thought here, but have you noticed the bravery of the sidewalk/city pigeons in recent years?

They really have become almost immune to us human beings. Whereas in the good old days they would scatter in fear, if not shame, if you got within fifty feet of them—now these attitude-infested pigeons barely acknowledge our existence, especially if they are munching on a good piece of found food.

Yes, they used to scatter in fear. Now they will ignore you until the very last second. Until you are right on top of them.

Pigeons clearly have developed a new attitude over the years. I call this phenomenon "Pigeonous Eruptous." I think scientists have a different fancy name for this, but clearly through evolution and time, pigeons are getting more used to us humans.

We don't scare pigeons like we used to. I believe you could make the same comparison to a disease fighting off certain vaccines. The disease simply "gets used to" the vaccine. Or maybe a better example would be how mosquitos adapted to mosquito repellant over the years and are not affected by the spray nearly as much as they used to be.

Same concept. Call it the "adaptation effect."

Indeed, pigeons have evolved in their relationship with us Homo sapiens. This evolution has clearly come with a very pronounced lack of respect. Basically they don't care about us as much. We are not to be feared as we used to be. They have become very laissez-faire pigeon-esque. Almost like a teenager dealing with his parents. In one ear and out the other. Ya…ya…ya…whatever…. Can I go now?

Again, no dramatic social commentary here. Nothing really to worry about…except…

If the trend continues into the next generation, as I fully expect it will, human beings will literally have to start sharing the sidewalk with pigeons. Our fine-feathered friends will not be flying away in fear as they have in the past. Pigeon and man will walk the same pathways through life.

Sadly, those pathways may be inundated with bird droppings, as I don't think this "evolution" advancement will include pigeons using public restrooms. (Possible invention idea? See immediately previous topic.)

And remember, it may start with sidewalks, but it surely will move on to other common areas we have controlled and walked through so freely without even thinking. So, young readers…be prepared. Be very prepared. The pigeons are slowly, but surely moving in.

And what happens with generations beyond if the trend continues? Who knows? But for possible end results, please reference: Hitchcock comma Alfred, nee movie—*The Birds*.

With that lovely thought…. Have a nice day!

So True

At every party there are basically two kinds of people—
those who want to leave early and those who don't.
The problem is, they are usually married to each other.

"Life is too short to play chess."
~Henry James Byron

Remember, there is only one thing between
you and the top of the company ladder.
The ladder.

I once knew a guy who was so lazy,
he wouldn't even take the path of least resistance.

Some minds are like concrete:
thoroughly mixed and permanently set.

"I always thought the world was divided into only two kinds of
people—those who think the world is divided into two kinds of
people and those who don't."
~Molly Irvins
As quoted in the Asheville, North Carolina, *Citizen-Times*

Lesson Learned

Most people learn about the laws of economy from reading the paper, the stock market, economics class, maybe business class.

For me it was the Hostess Suzy Q.

Every year during my four years in high school, at our cafeteria I would get the exquisite taste sensation brought to us by the fine folks at the Hostess Cake Company known as the "Suzy Q." Two moist chocolate cake buns, with sinfully good white cream filling.

Hostess was most known for their famous Twinkies. But to me, the Twinkie was vastly overrated. The Suzy Q just never got its proper recognition. Always in the shadows of Lord Twinkie.

But this twin chocolate cake sensation with the white cream filling took a backseat to no dessert. Trust me on this.

Sure as can be…I learned simple economics from watching the amount of cream filling in my Suzy Q shrink each and every year. Freshman year, the thing was bursting with white trans-fat delight. It was a puffed-up sensation. The José Canseco of desserts. By sophomore year, not so much. Still pretty good, but a definitive decline in the amount of filling. Junior year, the cream filling was barely noticeable, and by senior year you had to send out a search party to find that whipped cream delight.

You can talk all you want about the law of diminishing returns, getting by with less, stock market analysis, and economic downturns. I learned all I needed to know about our shrinking economy, and the weakening of product quality, during my four years in our high school cafeteria.

I am over it now. Crushing lunchtime disappointment clearly in the rearview mirror. But it was a painful real life lesson at the time.

Moment of silence, please, for my beloved Hostess Suzy Q?... Thank you. I feel a little better now.

Jon Cohn

The Need to Read

Everyone has their own list of favorite books…and there is clearly a wide range of likes and dislikes here. But I give to you, for the first time, my CSR Awards for literary greatness. CSR—my brand-name label for "Can't Stop Reading"—which really is the best sign of a good book.

Before doing so, I would like to give an honorary CSR Lifetime Achievement Award to the fine folks at CliffsNotes. This wonderful yellow- and black-looking pamphlet saved me many hours of frustration, analysis, and actual thinking back in my somewhat subversive high school and junior high days.

By deciphering the key points of most major novels—especially the ones teachers assigned us to read, and cutting through the author's tone, style, and depth while giving us the nuts and bolts of the story—we were able to complete every homework assignment required. At least enough to do a book report on. And in a minimum amount of time.

Taking a five-hundred-page novel and breaking it down for us in just twenty-four easy-to-read pages? Brilliant. Absolutely brilliant.

I'm not sure if today's young students are aware of what CliffsNotes are, or even their great and storied history—probably not because of the Internet—but believe me, they were a lifesaver for many of us.

And now…the coveted CSR Awards for the best five books of all time, as voted by this esteemed panel of one.

1. *Tuesdays with Morrie*: the *only* book I have ever read three times (probably more to come). Mitch Album's novel about his time spent with the elderly dying Morrie has more simple wisdom on life in one page than many novels do in five hundred.

2. *Exodus*: Maybe the first novel I actually read without using CliffsNotes! Incredible story told so eloquently. Lasting impact, for sure. Been a long time. I need to read this one again.

3. *Unbroken*: Lauren Hildebrand's remarkable book about Olympic sprinter, turned war hero, turned prisoner of war, turned born-again Christian Louis Zamparini is incredibly well-researched. And the story? Simply an amazing example of human perseverance and refusal to give in to odds that surely would have sunk most of us. Any one of the four parts—his childhood from troubled kid to Olympic sprinter, forty-six days in the Pacific Ocean on a raft after a plane crash, his tortured days in Japanese prison camps during WWII, or his return to normal life and its many struggles when back on U.S. soil—could have made for great books by themselves. Together? A classic read of epic proportions.

4. *Boys in the Boat*: This one surprised me. Never knew anything or had any particular interest in the sport of rowing before embarking on this book. But I got sucked in early and often and didn't come up for air until weeks later. A true story about the Olympic medal–winning University of Washington rowing team. The personal story of one of the rowers, Joe Rantz, is just as riveting.

5. *Born to Run*: Never expected it, but this book stunned me. It was a CSR (Can't Stop Reading) instant hit. Just an incredible story of running, mountains, and a tribe of runners that compete in some of the most grueling races known to man. Completely

unexpected, but one of the best reads ever. Even for the non-runner.

6. *New Rules*: Political satirist Bill Maher nails it on a regular basis in this book. And he does it all with a great sense of humor. A series of thoughts, opinions, and ideas all written in short paragraph form, which, if you can get past the crude language and the "in your face" style, has so much truth in it, it hurts. If you can laugh at yourself, and our society, and even be engaged in thinking about how we can do it better, then keep this baby on your nightstand. Guarenteed, you will go to sleep with a smile on your face.

Got your own CSR (Can't Stop Reading) nominations? Email them to us at jcsportsandtees@aol.com, and we may compile a top literary list for STUFF readers.

Quiet Time

A guy is crossing the street, and he gets suddenly run over
by one of those mobile book libraries.
He is lying in the street screaming in pain.
The first guy to come to his rescue looks at him and goes,
"Shhhh…"

A man stops another man in the street and tells him,
"I haven't eaten for five days!"
The other man says,
"Wow, I wish I had your willpower."

Money can't buy happiness…
but it does make unhappiness a lot easier to live with.

A guy bought a parrot.
The parrot talked. But it never said, "I'm hungry."
So it died.

Chalk Talk

Not sure what it was. And as far I can tell, I am a party of one here, but I absolutely loved writing on the chalkboard as a kid.

There was just something about the teacher writing on the chalkboard in the classroom that appealed to me. Can't explain it. Maybe some psychologist could take a crack at it—but it doesn't really matter, and I might not want to hear the analysis.

I think chalk and the chalkboard is part of the reason I went into coaching—just so I could write plays up on the chalkboard. For some kids, getting a bicycle or a radio was the greatest present they got as a kid. For me, it was a box of different-colored chalk. Truth be told, the colored chalk was second next to a complete box set of baseball cards. That, for me as a kid, was about as good as it got.

For some kids, getting in trouble at school and having to write "I will not tease Susie" a hundred times up on the blackboard was pure punishment. For me? It was nirvana.

It's Been Nice Knowing You

It's been real—but isn't it time to eliminate change (the cash kind) from our modern-day society?

Pennies, nickels, dimes, quarters…I mean, fellas, you have had a good run, but with expenses as they are today, do we really need you?

Just round it up to the nearest dollar. Save us all the pain.

We older folks all have some wonderful memories, no doubt. When you leave penny, nickel, dime, quarter, you may be gone, but you definitely won't be forgotten.

All good things must come to end, although we will need something to replace "flipping a coin" for sporting events or other decisions that require the almighty "flip."

P.S. Whoever said change is inevitable—was wrong.

Handy Andy

Some interesting words of wisdom from Andy Rooney—television commentator:

"The best classroom in the world is at the feet of an elderly person."

"Life is like toilet paper.
The closer you get to the end…the faster it goes."

"One should keep their words soft and tender,
because tomorrow you may have to eat them."

"Everybody wants to live a long life—
but no one wants to get old."

"*Vegetarian*—an old Indian word meaning 'lousy hunter.'"

"I don't like food that is too carefully arranged.
It makes me think the chef is spending too much time
arranging and not enough time cooking.
Hey, if I wanted a picture, I'd buy a painting."

Decisions, Decisions

Here's something interesting to think about. And it may be truer than we want to admit.

Let's say scientific research discovers, through some long and extensive research, that cell phone use can lead to brain damage. Say the studies that come out are similar to the early studies in the sixties and seventies regarding smoking and the likely correlation that cigarettes can cause cancer.

Here is the question.

If cell phones were found to have some link to brain cancer—how hard would it be for people to stop using them? How addicted to cell phone use are all of us? Could we stop using them if the science said it could be health-threatening (just like cigarettes)?

I hope we never have to find out...but I wonder how strong our addiction to the cell phone is and whether we could stop if it held the same health risk as nicotine?

Not sure anyone knows the answer, but it is interesting to contemplate. Would it be harder or easier than five decades ago, when they told us smoking was dangerous for our health?

Let's hope we never have to actually answer this one...but it is interesting to think about.

The Times, They Are a'Changing

This list displayed on the Internet gives a pretty good example of how times have changed for our Baby Boomer generation... not necessarily for the better. (Don't laugh, Millennials—your time is coming!) For instance:

1975: Going to a hip new joint
2015: Receiving a new hip joint

1975: Hoping for a BMW
2015: Hoping for a BM

1975: Rolling Stones
2015: Kidney Stones

1975: Screw the system
2015: Upgrade the system

1975: Disco
2015: Costco

1975: Acid rock
2015: Acid reflux

1975: Passing the driving test
2015: Passing the eye test

It ain't easy getting old—but then again, it does beat the alternative.

Hail to the Stooges!

A STUFF book just wouldn't be complete without a proper salute to the great ones—the Three Stooges.

Moe, Larry, Curly, and Shemp were a big influence in my younger years (which probably explains at least some of the strange theories in this book), and they were absolute comic geniuses of the physical variety.

I always tell people that Curly was the greatest comedian of all time, and here is why. The things he did—the strange sounds, silly antics, wacky comments, physical absurdities—could not possibly have been scripted by even the funniest of writers.

Curly was comedy free fall at its finest. When he got on a roll, it was like watching Baryshnikov in action. Truly poetry in motion of the most comedic kind.

But don't kid yourselves, the Stooges could be violent. They were always pounding away at each other, ripping out hair, poking at eyes, and of course, Moe would specialize in using basic mechanical tools (hammer, wrench, saw) to belt Curly and Larry around. The stuff got pretty violent, and the best was the sound effects to go along with it. (The crunching sound as Moe twisted a crowbar around in Curly's nose was particularly memorable.)

Somewhere around age ten, me and my brothers were banned from watching the Stooges because of the violence factor. I went eight very long, difficult, and trying years without my Moe, Larry, Curly, and Shemp fix.

Basketball games, eight track players, and the discovery of the opposite sex proved worthy distractors. But I still missed my Stooges.

Finally, in college, there was a *Three Stooges* film festival on campus. I figured by now, in my late teens and early twenties, they would seem childish and immature and probably not even funny anymore. But what the heck? For old times' sake I checked it out.

Surprisingly, any maturing I did do over those eight years did not take the comedic sting out of the Stooges. They were funnier than I remembered them as a kid! They had a whole adult level to their humor that I had never appreciated back in my younger years. I was hooked once again.

I have read three books over the years on the Stooges. Done a little research, as well. If Alex Trebek and the gang ever come out with a Three Stooges' *Jeopardy* contest, I'll be right there at the front of the line.

And I am proud to say, I did my fatherly duty, as my two boys were introduced to the Stooges at a young age—and both liked them as much as I did. We shared some good laughs together—just us men, with Mom in the other room completely oblivious to the humor of the Stooges.

At any rate, I did want to give a nod to my guys somewhere during the course of the book. Thanks for the laughs guys!

Oh…and one other benefit I almost forgot. You could always look at Shemp…and then look at yourself in the mirror—and always feel pretty good about your own physical appearance. (Nyuk, nyuk…." Why certainly!)

One of Life's True Mysteries

Life is full of little mysteries. One of them to me is who, and or what, is the Cornish hen? I get perplexed by the strangest of things, I admit. I am easily confused, but still… What the heck is this strange food item I only see at special events?

I haven't been to too many weddings in recent years, but during my friends' wedding years it seemed that a common food to serve was the dreaded Cornish hen. I could never understand this. Plus it always looked to me like they had just killed and stuffed it minutes before serving it with a rice pilaf. I swear, that hen was staring back at me.

So my questions are plentiful:

Why do we only eat Cornish hens at weddings or banquets?

What is a Cornish hen?

Is it really Cornish, and if so what does being Cornish mean?

Where do they breed this rare species?

Why don't regular restaurants ever offer the Cornish hen on their menus?

…and finally, why is that hen always staring at me when I am about to take it apart to eat? This is quite disturbing and can ruin the otherwise fine glass of champagne I am washing it down with.

At any rate, these are the hard questions we bring up here in the STUFF book. This is hard-hitting editorial here, and I need answers.

Jon Cohn

Laugh Trax

The good things in life: peace, happiness, good health,
and soft tissue paper—not necessarily in that order.

If four out of five people suffer from diarrhea…
does that mean the other one enjoys it?

Do infants enjoy infancy as much as adults enjoy adultery?

Remember, light travels faster than sound.
That is why some people appear to be bright until
you actually hear them speak.

One teenager to another:
"What are you doing?"
"Oh, I just woke up from a nap,
and now I'm playing some video games."
"Okay, you wanna come over and hang out?"
"No, I can't. I'm at work."
~*Zits* comic strip

When you can, borrow money from a pessimist.
That way he won't expect it back.

Remember:
In just two days, tomorrow will be yesterday.

215

Old Lesson Remembered

had a teacher once who told us this: Don't underestimate the signifi-cance of the first word when you are describing something. It was something I remembered for a long time, particularly because of the example she gave.

Try these two descriptions of a person, and see how the tone changes based on the first word in describing them.

1. He was a warm, hardworking, quiet, introspective, tough, and demanding man.

2. He was a cold, hardworking, quiet, introspective, tough, and demanding man.

Just the first descriptive word is different. But the meaning and por-trayal of the person is completely changed. Again—just a small lesson one day in a fifth-grade classroom…but one I always remembered.

XVXRYONX IN THX GROUP IS NXXDXD

read this many years ago, and I still think it is the best example yet of the importance of working together, and the importance of each person in the group.

It goes like this...

Xvxn though my typxwritxr is an old modxl, it works quitx wxll xxcxpt for onx of thx kxys. I havx wishxd many timxs that it workxd pxrfxctly. It is trux thxrx arx forty-six kxys that function wxll xnough, but just onx kxy not working makxs thx diffxrxncx.

Somxtimxs it sxxms to mx that our group is somxwhat likx my typxwritxr...not all thx kxy pxoplx arx working propxrly.

You may say to yoursxlf, "Wxll, I am only onx pxrson. It won't makx much diffxrxncx." But you arx...thx group, to bx xffxctivx, nxxds thx activx participation of xvxry pxrson.

So thx nxxt timx you think you arx only onx pxrson, and that your xffort is not nxxdxd, rxmxmbxr my typxwritxr and say to yoursxlf, "I am a kxy pxrson, and nxxdxd vxry much!"

Another Installment of RAH RAH (Real American Heroes)

Time to add a little spirit and pep here, as we give out a couple of RAH RAHs to our underrated and undetected list of…drumroll, please…**R**eal **A**merican **H**eroes.

I would like to nominate two very quiet, but definitely worthy candidates to our RAH RAH list. We often pass them by (literally), and maybe give a quick glance—but how many of us stop and think how truly heroic they are?

So here it is. A quick bouquet of kudos thrown the way of the many stroke and accident victims we see walking at the fitness center or using the outdoor running tracks—all who are just "getting back on the horse" and learning to walk again, *and*…for the friend or family member or paid professionals who guide them through it.

I have seen and witnessed these fine folks in action many times. Too often I have passed them, not stopping to think about the difficulties they must be going through.

For the stroke or accident victim, it has to be incredibly difficult. In many cases they were the person racing around the track, or moving along in sprightly fashion with a fast pace and confident walk—all before a sudden stroke or accident, almost always unexpected, set them back to the very basics. Now what once came so easy, becomes literally a step-by-step battle. Fighting at times just to make one lap. Watching others, as they once were, easily and healthily moving past them.

How frustrating that must be. And how difficult it must be to keep going. But onward they push…step by step, unbalanced lunge by unbalanced lunge, occasionally reaching for the bar, and then, after a brief rest and usually with dedicated encouragement, bravely continuing on. Truly inspirational to observe…if we actually stop to do so.

RAH RAHs also go out to the people who urge them on. The patience, encouragement, and positive attitude of the people I see helping the stroke or accident victim is inspirational. It can't be easy for them, either. The pace is painfully slow. Improvements are only miniscule each day. Their time commitment, significant.

But they soldier on, these assistants. They may be family members, friends, or sometimes a paid professional, but whoever they are—they stay with their patient doggedly. I watch them. And I admire greatly their dedication.

Usually it is the same person each and every day. It must take an amazing amount of patience. To me it is a true test of loyalty and human compassion that they continue this task in support of the stroke or accident victim. They are as inspirational to watch as the victims themselves.

So, kudos to both of you.

Every time I get slightly upset, as I am sure many of us have—hey, we're human!—on a track when it gets backed up a bit and you see part of it is due to the slow-paced individuals on the inner ring of the track, I stop myself and just think how lucky I am—and more importantly, what a true yeoman's job of human effort they are performing.

May your steps get easier and faster in the future.

RAH RAHs, indeed…for each and every one of you.

The Obituary Wall

Here is an idea that I have found helpful. I tried to come up with a more creative name (which I am usually pretty decent at), but in this case I just couldn't. So I call it simply the "Obituary Wall."

I started this about five years ago in a rare moment of inspiration (nothing to do with the unintended coincidence of switching my favorite drink from a beer to bourbon on the rocks—straight-up, no water). I do strongly wish I had started this idea earlier, because so many have passed and gone who were surely worthy of being put on the wall.

But, sadly, the list is growing.

Here is the way it works, and it is quite simple. When someone passes away, I keep on a sheet of paper (the Wall) their names, and then a few things about them I most remember. It could be a personality trait, a personal story, something they said, something they did, the way they went about their life, or maybe even the way they affected my life. A myriad of possibilities here—but don't overthink it. Keep it simple, and just write down a few things you will remember about this person.

The people you put on the wall can be anyone from close family members to famous people you never even met. They could be neighbors, or friends growing up, or someone you knew from your parents' generation. Anyone, really, who you remember with some level of feeling. Someone who may have touched you in some way.

Now you have a list you can periodically look at. I have found it a small, but very mentally cleansing activity to do so.

When you review the list, it may make you sad. It may make you smile. It may make you think. And maybe, just maybe, it will remind you of some things you should be doing or a certain way you should be acting in your own life. I know it has had that effect for me.

The "Obituary Wall" is just a thought. It may not work for many. But again, I have found this very useful—and I wish so much I would have started doing it many years ago so I would now have an extensive "Wall" to look back on for support and inspiration.

Life Comes Full Circle...Unfortunately

Success at 4 is not peeing in your pants.

Success at 12 is making friends.

Success at 16 is getting a driver's license.

Success at 20 is having sex.

Success at 35 is making money.

Success at 50 is making money.

Success at 60 is having sex.

Success at 70 is having a driver's license.

Success at 75 is having friends.

Success at 80 is not peeing in your pants.

(Source: Boardofwisdom.com)

Loud and Proud

The crying baby; the street preacher waxing poetic at abnormally high decibels as we walk by; the high-verbiage, way-too-friendly passenger who just happens to be sitting next to you in the airplane; the lovely moviegoer who decides to sit directly behind you and comment on the movie at almost every interval…

All examples of people clearly too loud for their own good.

It is interesting…our natural tendency is to be turned off by any of the above examples—or anyone, really, who steps beyond our verbal personal space and enters the high-decibel non-comfort zone. We tend to go in rejection mode, and for the most part, this is usually a pretty rock-solid policy.

But there are exceptions…

I remember a movie I saw a while back. I can't remember the name, but it had one scene in which Jerry Stiller and Anne Meara, the famous married comedy team, were trying to smuggle something past airport security. The movie was a comedy, so this was all done in humor, and it was done back in the nineties—so airport security certainly was not nearly what it is now.

The wife, Anne Meara, was trying to figure out sneaky ways to get past security with their recently acquired stolen goods. She came up with a multitude of ingenious ideas. But husband, Jerry Stiller, had a different idea. A much simpler way.

He told his wife, "Let's be as loud and obnoxious as possible. Nobody likes or pays attention to loud people, security won't want to deal with us, and they will just quickly escort us through."

So that is exactly what they did. Meara and Stiller—who mastered the husband-and-wife-nagging comedy routine—proceeded to argue with each other loudly, complaining about the bags, complaining about the long line, complaining about security…you get the idea.

Sure enough, Special Forces came over to quiet them down, as customers were getting perturbed by the two. They brought them over to a special entrance area, calmed them down, and quickly pushed the two elderly, clearly harmless, yet rambunctious couple through onto the walkway so as not to create any more disturbances or delays.

Off went the happy old couple—of course, with all of their stolen goods. And the quick, glancing smile at each other as they moved on through said it all.

It's a classic example of how those who are the loudest are often ignored the most. And as I said before, for the most part—probably as well they should.

But there are exceptions. And sometimes we can miss out on something good, just because it is, on first appearance, too loud! And maybe a bit too proud.

I bring to you as witness number one (of my one-witness argument here), none other than TV preacher and evangelist Mr. Joel Osteen.

Let that set in for just a second... That's right, I am throwing some kudos the way of a TV preacher.

Thank goodness this book is not a phone, as I am sure most of you would hang up at this point in the conversation...but hang with me here. And as an added bonus, I promise to you I will not be asking for a monetary donation at the end of this segment.

Now, most of us—myself definitely included—immediately cringe upon hearing about any TV preacher. We have heard the stories of Jim Bakker and Tammy Faye and what happened with them, but even more so, we don't like anyone preaching at us loudly and proudly, and especially doing so broadcast over the TV.

It is a natural tendency toward aversion here. Completely understandable, really.

But...over the past ten or fifteen years, I have, on occasion, while flipping channels on the old TV on a Sunday morning, come across Osteen at the pulpit. I have to admit, on rare occasion I stopped to listen, and really without thinking about it too much, I would come away surprisingly impressed. Not like some of the others I have heard. His messages hit home, and they made sense. I stopped to ponder a bit…and then I would move on to my morning ESPN highlights—or if it was during the season when my beloved Cubs were losing (oops—I mean, playing), I might search instead for a good *Three Stooges* rerun.

By the by…as a complete side note here…WARNING—going from TV preaching immediately over to Moe, Larry, and Curly is a dangerous transition! It should really only be done under adult supervision and only in the direct comfort of your own home.

Anyhoo…here is what happened. Most recently, the Joel Osteen channel was added to Sirius radio. I do a fair amount of driving around in the car, so I will listen to many different Sirius stations. Along with my Barry Manilow station and my country music preset and, of course, twelve different sports stations…I decided to hook up the Osteen channel as one of my presets (sorry, Home Repair Helpers—but something had to go).

On occasion, I started listening to Osteen and the replays of some of his messages, which they play on the station. As I said before, I am a pretty practical listener, not easily taken in by scheme or trickery—or religious overtones.

But the more I listened—this time not in snippets, but to large chunks of his speech—the more impressed I became.

Now, keep in mind, as I have already explained, I am non-religious in a formal sense. The dedicate-yourself-to-God, believe-in-Jesus, and look-for-your-salvation messages have just never resonated with me. And further keep in mind that I have never been a fan of the TV evangelists and/or preachers.

But I started to listen to Osteen with an open mind. His messages (do I have to say here…"I admit"?) were very often right-on. They were practical. They were motivating. They were real life. They were inspirational. But most importantly, they were done in ways not to make anyone feel left out or insignificant for "not believing."

Osteen does not holler and shout. He does not scream from the pulpit. He adds religious context and does include God and Jesus, but never in a sense that it puts down those who might not believe.

But most importantly, he gives you suggestions, ideas, and motivation that can help you in the way you approach your life. I have taken some of the lessons to heart and tried to put them to real use.

Moreover, his talking style—which appears to be done without notes—is brilliant. His speech delivery is like watching Michelangelo sculpt, Rembrandt paint, or maybe Michael Jordan shoot a jump shot. Just a wonderful, smooth, but not burdensome speaking style done with a sense of humor and, of course, great belief and conviction.

Now, the reason for me mentioning this is not to convert anyone to the "Joel Osteen church." Least of all myself.

I simply want to point out that in our natural aversion to avoid anything a bit too loud, or a bit too overbearing, we may automatically turn off something that actually could be of interest or help. Not often, I admit. Usually loud and way too proud—be it a TV commercial or a preacher on the street, is turn-off mode well spent.

But occasionally, just on rare occasions, there may be something really valuable, or enjoyable, or simply interesting, from what appears to be an overbearing person.

So, if we let ourselves open up occasionally, or at least not turn away too quickly from these types of people, maybe—just maybe—we will find ourselves not regretting it.

It worked for me with Joel Osteen, TV preacher and evangelist. Who woulda thunk it?

Now, if you are interested in sending in money to help…

Oh, What a Tangled Web We Weave

There simply is no explanation. But we all know this to be true. It is one of the great mysteries of life—one that unites all of us—young, old, people of all colors, of all religions. One could argue this may be one of the only things we all agree upon, across all civilizations and societies.

What is this phenomenon we speak of?

You put a set of lights away (Christmas or any other kind)—neatly—for the season, and you open them up again next year. What do we get? Every time? A tangled mess.

Somehow, over the eleven months of storage and quiet silence and solitude, these lights slowly but surely envelop into each other. Slowly but surely they loop and twist and turn and tangle. How or when this happens we do not know. It could be in the light of day…it could be in the deep depths of the dark evening hours…but somehow, someway—no matter how neatly we put them away—the lights will find a way to become a tangled mess by the time we open them next year.

It is, indeed, one of the great mysteries of life. Unraveling this phenomenon, along with the stars and the universe, will surely be left to generations in the future…

We can only wonder in amazement what they will discover…

Follow Up

On a related note, our next STUFF book will discuss lost socks in the dryer: myth or legend?
(Wow, what a teaser!)
Other possible STUFF topics being considered:

1. STUFF...people might be thinking to themselves at a political debate (part tragedy/part comedy)

2. STUFF...we probably forgot, but really should remember (for the over-sixty age group)

3. STUFF...not to say at your kid's parent-teacher meeting (I am an expert on this one)

4. STUFF...we probably shouldn't be eating (nineteen volumes' worth)

5. STUFF...to think about in today's dating scene (special single and married person editions available)

6. STUFF...the technology-challenged need to know about today's technological world

   (Somebody please write this book!)

7. STUFF...we can't think of right now—but that should be in a book (self-serving—sorry!)

Do you have any ideas for a future STUFF book? Any and/or all ideas are welcome at jcsportsandtees@aol.com.

Hello? Anybody Listening?

This has to stop!

I continue to be amazed by the number of "organizations" that still require you to give out your Social Security number.

Just recently, I have been asked to give out my Social Security number for a son enrolling in a junior college class, for a clothing store credit card, and on a housing application for son number two at his university.

Seriously? In this day and age? You ask for my Social Security number for enrolling in a summer class at a junior college? You need to know my Social Security number to secure housing? You need my Social Security number for a retail store credit card?

No...No...No...No...and...more *no!*

We are not breaking ground here in telling people that in this day and age of cybersecurity and internet fraud that you do not—repeat, *do not*—give out your Social Security number to anybody...except maybe on a tax return, or some other official application from our fine government.

This includes, by the way, job applications. The key word here being *application*. For you to apply, they do not need your Social Security number. Once you are hired? Different story. For tax purposes, this will be needed. But not before.

The casuality of asking people for their Social Security numbers (which, if in the wrong hands, can basically tell everything about you and your bank account) amazes me.

As I said at the beginning, this needs to stop. Pronto.

My word to the wise: If they ask you to give your Social Security number—fight it! It is a hassle, but don't give in. Try to educate them on the reason they should not be asking.

This will be a long battle, folks—only to be won by all of us banding together. Every little bit of resistance helps. Join in on the fight to protect your security! Remind one and all that they *cannot* and *should not* ask for your Social Security number! For any reason.

Thank you for your help and…

Remember, the moving of a giant rock begins by taking away one small stone at a time. Or something like that.

Words to Smile By

Keep the dream alive...hit the snooze button.

A man's computer password was
"*WinnieDopeySleepyMickey*BugsBunnyMinnieHappyWoody
WoodpeckerWashingtonDC."
Asked why he had chosen that as his password,
the gentleman responded,
"I thought it was supposed to be eight characters and a capital."

You ever hear the joke about the dyslexic guy who walks into a bra?

A blind man married a blind woman.
Their kids were really nothing to look at.

Legally it is questionable; morally it is disgusting;
personally, I like it!

Back in the day, United Airlines sued Continental Airlines.
The reason:
The proud bird with the golden tail crapped all over the friendly skies.

"Hey, have you taken a bath lately?"
"No, why? Is one missing?"

Photographer's Wonderful Wisdom

In this day and age when photographers and reporters literally put their lives on the line to give us, the readers, the best possible look (both in pictures and print) of some of the atrocities that may be happening abroad, it certainly is worth giving them their due accolades.

Listen to the words of *Time* magazine photographer James Nachtwey, upon receiving the National Magazine Awards highest individual honor. The award-winning photographer explains his craft and purpose to the audience:

"We navigate dangers, endure hardships and get our hearts broken by what we witness, over and over again, because we believe that people's opinions matter, that our society cannot function properly without the information we provide and without the stories we tell."

"Our work is aimed at our readers' best instincts—generosity, compassion, a sense of right from wrong, a sense of identification with others on a human level, across cultures, beyond the borders of nationality, and perhaps most importantly, the refusal to accept the unacceptable."

That's strong stuff. Simple, but really strong.

Reread. Rinse. Repeat.

Unfortunately, This Is True

You may have heard via joke or simple small talk, the old axiom that it is always the older gentlemen in the men's locker room who are the ones that all too often are walking around completely, unabashedly naked.

Unfortunately, I can say after experiencing a number of fitness and gym locations over recent years…this old proverb is all too true.

Very unfortunate. But true.

It really is *not* a good look! It absolutely becomes an impossible erasure from the pictured memory log of the young brain, where the "photo delete" button does not work quite so decisively.

To understand this "open" locker room attitude is to understand it as a generational thing. It follows in order similar (sort of) to the evolution of man. A step-by-step, generation-by-generation gradual change in locker room mores.

Let us examine.

In our parents' generation, the unabashed locker room uncovering was commonly accepted. The casual stark-naked walk, browsing and lounging around the locker room in full bare regalia, was no big deal. It was the way of the world, and don't even get me started on the steam rooms—we could start a whole new chapter or even a book here.

The following generation—the Baby Boomers? A bit more modest, definitely. The invention of the locker towel, I believe, can be attributed to this fine group.

Next, the Gen Xers and the Millennials? They were even more prone to covering up in the locker room. I believe Neil Armstrong said it best: "One small step for modesty, one giant step for paranoid males"…or something like that.

And the young generation of kids today? They rarely even shower in public. They have gone to the other extreme. They don't undress in public. They go in complete coverup mode. Towels are used to wipe the forehead, and that is about it.

Maybe with the today's youth, it is because of all the media and social outlets that have publicized horrible stories and horrible pictures of a variety of incidents. The advent of the Internet and, in particular instant pictures via cell phone, and the increased use of social media can bring modesty to even the strongest amongst us.

But the older generation refuses to break here. Their locker room tradition reigns supreme. They tread proudly along in full unclothed regalia, oblivious to the changing mores of the generations postceding them. And thus the unfortunate aged naked parade marches on in locker rooms across America.

I know it is a tradition for their generation. And I am all about continuing great traditions.

But this is one that could—and should—end. Immediately. Please. Thank you in advance for your cooperation.

Something Borrowed

Couldn't resist throwing in a few Jeff Foxworthy "You might be a redneck if…"

1. Your high school fight song was "Dueling Banjos."

2. You think a family reunion is a good place to "meet chicks."

3. Your mother lists "ammo" on her Christmas gift list.

4. You call sixth grade your "senior year."

5. You list as "career goals" to own a bait stand.

6. You have gone hunting on a tractor.

7. Motel 6 turns off their lights when you arrive.

8. Rather than drinking the wine at church, you "bring your own."

9. You call your wife the better half, because she "better have" dinner on the table.

10. Your favorite Mexican food is Doritos.

11. You think "loading the dishwasher" means getting your wife drunk.

12. Your dad walks you to school—because you're both in the same grade.

13. Your junior/senior prom had to provide day care.

The Sand Pebbles of Time

On a completely non-significant point, without going all scientific and all molecular on us, can you name a finite number larger on this planet earth than the number of granules of sand?

I struggle to. And I have always been amazed at the thought of what the number could be.

Think about this. You pick up one handful of sand and start to count. Just one little handful. Even that small handful is well into the thousands. Now imagine how many handfuls there are in just a small area of a beach. And then look at the entire beach and think how many handfuls there may be. And then think of all the beaches in this country, and then in the world. That is a whole lot of handfuls!

I don't know how you figure it out—and I don't really need an exact or estimated number—but I challenge anyone to give me something on earth that would be a larger number. Something finite and definitive like the granules of sand.

No relevant importance here. Just a weird and random thought.

Email us at jcsportsandtees@aol.com if you can come with other like numbers (again of something finite and tangible)—and we will see what interesting responses we get.

Confusing?

Is anyone else hving trouble switching from regular writing to txting? And then from txting back to reg writing? We now txt so much, that much of r writing bcomes the abbreviated version we use in txt.

BTW if u r under age 20 u can skp 2 the next item. This prbly doesn't affect u.

I njoy txting. It is convenient and does save time. But it also devlps bad habits that can affect u when it is time to write 4 sthing officl or imprtnt.

I am sure the editor and proofreader of this book will agree. I certainly wouldn't want to b an English teacher thse days. How do they grde paprs?

"TRAP"—A New Political Party for the Best of Us and the Rest of Us

Alright, time once again to tackle another light subject—this time the creation of a brand-new political party...just to change things up a bit.

That's right, right here in your friendly STUFF book, we give you an alternative to our two-party system, which, we all have to agree, has gone stale if not rancid in recent years.

So we bring to you, in full living color, our alternative to this two-party poopfest, and we call our new concept TRAP (The Reasonable American Platform).

The "TRAP COALITION" or "PLATFORM" (we are getting rid of the word *party*) is based on the fact that it seems for most of us, the current political parties don't really represent us. They have gone to the extremes on many issues, and in many cases they get so lost in the inner eye of the hurricane of political musings that common sense and logical thought processes get pushed aside.

So, again, we present to you: The **R**esponsible **A**merican **P**latform (**TRAP**).

We believe there is a strong and silent majority of Americans who have a core of basic beliefs that are *not* being represented now. Understanding there might not be perfect consensus in this platform of ideas, we are confident, as a whole, that it represents a large majority.

Following are some our basic beliefs:

1. There is a great divide in this country between those who have and those who have not. This "divide" has become way too great. It needs to be lessened. There is something fundamentally and humanely wrong

with some people making or having millions of dollars while others, who are working hard, barely are able to get by. We are not talking about making everything and everyone even. We are not talking drastic changes (please stop shouting "socialism"!) But simply put, we do see the need to bring the two ends of people's lifestyles a bit closer. We believe that this is a simple, normal, natural human instinct to want to see this.

2. If it is an American company with headquarters here, all jobs should be done here, by people in this country. Period. Same concept for every other country. Companies from another country should create jobs for people in their own country. We would eliminate sending jobs overseas. Simple concept. Don't overthink. Company is here. Workers should be here. Same everywhere.

3. Abortion issue: Unlike most of what we see depicted in today's media on this sensitive topic—we see *both sides* of it. We struggle with all of those who are strongly opposed *or* strongly in favor! This is an extremely difficult and sensitive issue. We do not agree with those we see on TV and in the media who are angry and fighting for one side and attacking the other. TRAP is very sensitive here. We see arguments on both ends. It is a very tough issue that requires some pensive thought. In general, though, we lean slightly toward the woman's right to choose. We do feel we would largely support the woman's right to choose in the first three months of pregnancy, while, later in pregnancy, the last five months, we would not

advocate abortion. But there are so many issues at play here that really call for reasoned, middle-ground discussion. In short, our primary focus here is to stop the extreme positions on this topic, and at least attempt to understand and sympathize a bit with the opposite views in this very difficult issue.

4. Gay marriage issue: This should *not* be a difficult issue. Unlike the abortion issue, there is no struggle here. This is a pretty easy concept, we feel. Any two people, regardless of gender, if they are in love and want to commit to each other, should be able to get married. Period. Here we do not sympathize with both sides. It is a law whose time has long since come, and it should be passed immediately. Too many have suffered for too long. And needlessly, we might add. We sympathize (a bit) with those who struggle to hold on to the tradition of marriage being between a man and a woman only. But it is a tradition only…and one that has grown out of step with current society.

5. Raise the minimum wage. Significantly. We are not financial experts. We are not business experts. But we do feel strongly that in the current business structure of large corporations, the top executives' salaries and benefits have become way, way too excessive. And those on the lower end of the scale earn not nearly enough. Again, we are not talking perfect equality here, but clearly a more fair way to structure salaries. Everyone works hard to make a corporation successful. The top executive, all the way down to the service personnel—they all put in a hard day's work. And

they all should get a comfortable, livable salary. Top administrators should be paid well—they certainly deserve it...but not nearly the extravagant salaries and bonuses we see now. It has gotten way out of line! Pay executives a nice substantial salary, no problem. But stop the excess pay, complete with vacations, second and third homes, and unlimited travel expenses. And significantly raise the salaries of those in the lower and middle rungs of the company salary structure. Simple concept. But a very important one and very much at the core of the TRAP philosophy.

6. Lobbyists: This is simple, but strong. Get rid of the whole "lobbyist system." There should be no lobbyists! It has corrupted the political system. It has wasted money. It is influencing our elected officials in a negative way. It is a money in/money out system that makes both the lobbyist and the corporations they support wealthier and stronger...and gives less voice to the average non-represented American. It also continues to promote the incestuous relationship between politicians and large corporations, and feeds the "doing favors" way of business that has become all too familiar in today's political landscape. Again, so there is no confusion. We support the elimination of the entire "lobbyist" system.

7. Political campaigning: Major restructuring and major change in thought process here. Much less money and much less time should be spent on the "campaign trail." It has gotten completely out of control, and worse yet, has become somewhat of a farce and a caricature of what it originally was supposed

to be. Here is what we propose. Every candidate gets a certain amount of money for "campaigning." It should be a mere pittance of what is spent now. There should be no campaign contributions from big donors or corporations. Any money that people want to donate to campaigns should instead be directed to a reputable charity of their choice. A much better use of the money! Here is what we propose: Each candidate will prepare written position statements, with their ideas and thoughts on how they would govern. There will be certain set dates for a discussion (not a debate) between the candidates, where citizens can see and judge whom they would like to vote for. No commercials. No campaign tours. No phony speeches. No wasted money on a year-and-a-half-long campaign tour. Eliminate all that. (We would support candidate speeches in a controlled setting as part of the discussion groups.) And most of all…if a candidate is a current governor, senator, congressman, or president, We say this… do the job you were elected to do! Do not spend the good part of two years trying to get voters to elect you by visiting other states and campaign tours, etc. Do the job we elected you to do. Work hard in your own state or at the job you have, and that will encourage us to vote for you! And then, if you want to run for a higher office, at certain set times join that particular discussion group and put out your position statements. This would eliminate so much wasted time, money, and mindless posturing that goes on in our current out-of-control and fairly irrelevant political campaigns.

8. Politicians in general: We are gaining more and more support and interest in the idea of politics not being a career...but instead a service commitment. In other words, there should not be lifetime "politicians"...but instead respected and honorable people from the business community and other professions who want to serve a term as a representative in our political system. This approach would bring to politics a much more highly respected group of candidates.

8.5. The economy and debt crisis: It is a controversial subject right now...and a tough debate, no question. Similar to our views on abortion—we see both sides here and struggle with those who are on either extreme. But in general, our view is thus: We need to cut back spending significantly, and we need to raise taxes some. First...cut, cut, cut—where there is wasted spending—and there is much of it, no doubt! Do *not* cut programs that are supportive and legitimate for those among us who are financially struggling, or health-wise struggling, or in any way suffering in their current lifestyle. These legitimately supportive agencies should continue and not be cut back. We do need to cut the current growing tax breaks on large corporations. No loopholes. No tax attorneys. They should pay their fair share. We do need to raise taxes on the very wealthy. We may need to slightly raise taxes on the middle class—to help cut the deficit and to help continue the much-needed agencies that have been deemed legit and supportive. Now...

Having stated this…it should be mentioned that those of great wealth in this country have for the most part been incredibly generous in giving millions of dollars to wonderful charitable organizations and very helpful causes. And they have paid a large percentage of our American tax bill. We completely respect and acknowledge this. This is not stated enough when talking about those of great wealth. But the bottom line is, the wealth has become so top-heavy that those of great fortune can afford to give much more thorough taxes…and still enjoy all the comforts they could possibly ever want.

One final note on taxes. Simplify, Simplify, Simplify! Cut the tax form down to just a few pages. Eliminate most deductions (as well as the need for tax preparers!)

9.   Foreign policy/military issue: TRAP has a couple of thoughts here. 1) Safety and protection against those looking to disturb or terrorize should always be goal number one. 2) It is a global world now. Yes, the United States is a leading country in many ways, but we are just a part of the whole. The United States should not always be looked to for financial and military support. All countries need to work together. The NATO concept, in theory anyway, is a great one. Being a leader and a great example of freedom and progressive lifestyles is a wonderful thing, and a role the United States can assume…but again, we must remember that we are just one member of a larger organization (the world!), and we have to desist on those who think our country "stands above the rest." We don't. We are part of a global economy and a global political world, and hopefully without dictating as such, we can play a big part in keeping and promoting world peace and working together. But

we are all in it together. It truly is now, and it will become even more so in the future, a global world. For Thought: For those among us who are of the philosophy that we "must take care of our own first," we ask this, "Why is the life of someone in Charlotte, South Carolina, more valuable or more important than the life of someone in Egypt? Or...why is the life of a child in Butte, Montana, more important the life of a child in Somalia?" Think about this. Really think about this. And maybe, just maybe, it might change your perspective a bit, and help to understand why TRAP is concerned for making the world a better place for everyone—not just Americans.

10. Global warming/environment issue: Again, the TRAP movement does not pretend to be experts here. But clearly we need to make major strides toward becoming more environmentally conscious. We do feel that through our lifestyle here on earth, from technology to transportation, to industry, etc., that man has had an effect on the air we breathe, the water we drink, and weather conditions in general. So, for the most part, we do agree with science. Global warming is a legitimate concern, and one where action is deemed necessary. We do also, however, temper the concern somewhat. Drastic reaction to global warming at this time might not be needed. More study and research certainly need to be conducted. So, in general, we can best be described as concerned about global warming and willing to do actual and concrete things to help right now for sure—but with some natural hesitation to more excessive controls.

11. Education issue: Another difficult-to-solve problem, no doubt. One with many levels. Our basic points here are thus: 1) Today's kids learn differently than we did in the past. The world has changed much. Unfortunately, the current approach to school and its basic structure has not. A major redesigning of the "school day" is needed to include less of forty-five-minute classes, ringing bells, leaving for the next class, and a traditional math, science, and English curriculum. More curricula time needs to be spent on current events, creative thinking, specialized interests, physical education, health, motivation and morals training, etc. Too much to go into here…and still a tremendous work-in-progress…but suffice it to say, major changes are needed in the way we think of as traditional "school." 2) Teacher pay, funding, and emphasis on the education of our youth are still absolute top priorities. (Just keep those pensions under control!)

12. Immigration issue: In general, we do believe there needs to be an absolute tightening of the border and who can and can't come into this country. But for those men and women and children who have been here for a while, and who have been good citizens— which is the large, large majority—we would support a humanistic and non-insulting way for these hardworking people to become American citizens. We feel even the terms *illegal immigrant* or *illegals* dehumanizes these individuals.

13. Health care issue: Some thoughts here… We are open to private or government-run health services, but here is the key: 1) This must be an absolute top-

level priority (right behind national and world security). 2) Everyone must be covered and have some kind of protective health insurance. 3) Medical costs must come down! The fees are way too high! Doctors and hospitals, and we fully respect the tremendous work they do, simply are charging too much money. Sorry…but that is at the root of the problem. Beyond these two items, we are open for all improvements. But again, a simplified and effective health care system for all Americans is a major priority.

14. Gun control/the right to bear arms: It's not so complicated here. This issue is a classic example of why the TRAP platform is needed. Most people see this issue pretty clear. Here it is in plain terms: If registered and trained people want to keep a gun in their house, we suppose, with some reservations, it is okay. But rifles, or multi-gauged guns, or automatic firing weapons, or any other advanced weaponry, should *not* be sold to the general public at all! Get the automatic advanced weapons out of the gun stores! If people want to use them, they can do so by renting them at a shooting range—a *closely monitored* shooting range!

So, there you have it. Just a few of the basic items I think *most* people (understood, there will be some disagreement) would generally agree on. But more and more it doesn't seem like any of the "parties" really represent these views.

So if you want to jump on the TRAP bandwagon (right now there are plenty of good seats available), or if you want to comment further, as always jcsportsandtees@aol.com is the place to write.

A Cute Little Story

One day a little boy asked his dad, "What is politics?"

The dad said, "Well, son, let me try to explain it this way. I am the head of the family, so call me the president. Your mother is the administrator of the money, so we will call her the government. We parents are here to take care of your needs, so we will call you the people. The nanny, we will call her the working class. And your baby brother, let's call him the future. Now, think about that, and see if it makes sense."

So the little boy went off to bed thinking about what his dad had said. Later that night he heard his baby brother crying, so he got up to check on him. He found the baby had severely soiled his diaper. So the little boy went to his parents' room and found his mother, alone, sound asleep. Not wanting to wake her, he went to the nanny's room. Finding the door locked, he looked in the peephole and saw his father in bed with the nanny. He gave up and went back to bed.

The next morning, the little boy said to his father, "Dad, I think I understand the concept of politics now." The father said, "Good, son. Tell me in your own words what you think politics is about."

The little boy replied, "The president is screwing the working class, while the government is sound asleep. The people are being ignored, and the future is in deep s**t."

(Source: unijokes.com)

LFMD (Lesson from My Dad)

reat advice. Always walk tall. Head up. Confident (even when you're not quite so), and walk into a room with a smile on your face. Simple advice…but it works wonders.

Best Dessert Bar None

It's clearly controversial and impossible to decipher a winner, with nominations coming from literally all walks of life and locations. But...

...I am here to tell you about the best...the absolute best...sweet treat, hands-down, no questions asked.

I offer to you in all its full regalia and vivid color: the Cream Puffs at the Wisconsin State Fair.

You're probably staring right now with the same expression Dustin Hoffman did in *The Graduate* when he was told at a party that his future would be in [suspenseful pause]...plastics. In case you haven't guessed yet, that is a look I get quite often.

But, ladies and gentlemen, let me state thy case. I am here to tell you that Wisconsin State Fair cream puffs are "nirvana "in pastry form. Furiously fresh. Loaded with cold cream made of the real stuff, and a pastry on both ends that could melt in your mouth if you didn't eat it so fast.

Let me quickly paint the picture. At the fair (by the way, the best state fair of the fifty offered, although now with Colorado's new laws on marijuana, it might have some competition), they have a cream puff-making factory on-site. Right there in one of the huge festival halls. Big factory, tons of workers, all the machines going full-blast in a nice, cold, refrigerated area, and it is glass-enclosed so while you are waiting in line you can longingly watch the cream puffs being made.

The line moves quickly, but the wait is half the fun.

You move down the line and watch the puffs being made, and your mouth starts watering. Then you order. Then you pay. Then you find a table...and then, finally...you EAT THE CREAM PUFF.

Heaven on earth, my friends. Culinary ecstasy. They are almost obscenely fresh. And the taste is rich but mellow at the same time. It is not too sweet. That is the beauty of it.

Trust me on this. If nothing else in this book resonates, you must at some point—whatever it takes…fly, drive, walk, jog, or take a boat—you must try the Wisconsin State Fair cream puff.

And they come in dozen packs if you want so take some home for the family and neighbors. Your popularity scale back in the hood will rise significantly.

As I write this, it is only mid-March. Summer and festival season is still so far away. It pains me to think I must wait nearly three months for the next fix of my beloved Cream Puffs—Wisconsin-style.

Funny Food for Thought

"Liberalism is like a nude beach.
It is never quite as good once you have actually
seen it and experienced it."
~Dennis Miller

"The trouble with history is that there are way too many people involved."
~Novelist Nick Hornsby

If ignorance is bliss—then why aren't more people happy?

You know why Bunker Hill was so slippery?
'Cause the British were coming.

Latest survey breakthrough:
Three out of four people make up 75 percent of the population.

A guy spent 80 percent of his money on booze and women.
The other 20 percent he just wasted.

I give 100 percent during the week to my work:
Monday, 12 percent; Tuesday, 18 percent; Wednesday, 30 percent;
Thursday, 25 percent; and Friday, 15 percent.

Potential Children's Books that Didn't Quite Make it through Publishing

1. *Curious George and the High-Voltage Fence*

2. *Hammers, Screwdrivers, and Scissors: An I-Can-Do-It Book*

3. *Dad's New Wife, Robert*

4. *Fun Four-Letter Words to Know and Share*

5. *The Pop-Up Book of Human Anatomy*

6. *Strangers Always Have the Best Candy*

7. *Pop Goes the Hamster...and Other Great Microwave Games*

8. *Your Nightmares? They Could Be Real.*

9. *Why Can't Mr. Fork and Ms. Electrical Outlet Be Friends?*

10. *Daddy Drinks—Because You Cry*

Best Mental Therapy There Is

Step into my office for a minute as Dr. STUFF plays amateur psychologist for just a minute. Not to worry, as no needles, no prescriptions, and no bending over will be required. But here is my untrained observation.

Nothing can make you feel better than realizing how insignificant you are. This sounds completely opposite from normal logic, but let me explain in the following context.

There are two prime examples I can give here...

1. Lying down on a sleeping bag, look up at the sky on a beautiful clear summer night on a camping trip in, say, Northern Michigan. Look up and see the sky at its most spacious and most cavernous. It is endless, and it is amazing if you let the mind wander just a bit. You can see every star. You can clearly make out every constellation. You can even pretend you can make out the Milky Way, which I am convinced, by the way, is a figment of our imagination and scientists are just playing with us. With apologies to Barbra Streisand, you *can* literally see forever. Awe-inspiring on a nice, clear summer night.

2. Look out at the ocean or a very large lake or the Gulf of Mexico or any beautiful body of water that stretches endlessly into the horizon. See it from a beach or from a close-by building. But be close enough where you can hear the waves and look out into the endless stream of blue/green.

Either of those two visions is truly amazing.

When you look up at the highway of the skyway or the endless waterways of the ocean, you feel their vastness and realize what a giant and unknown universe there is around us. And—here is the key—by seeing this "eternalness of nature," it makes you realize how unimportant and small we really are in the vast scope of things.

Strangely, if you let it, this realization can actually make you feel good. You can begin to realize, *Maybe I shouldn't be worrying about so many small things* (that in our lives become big things if we let them). The understanding that I am only here in this...whatever it actually is...for a very short time. So...

Stop worrying so much. All of our daily distractions and worries and concerns, for the most part, in the big scope of things (see the ocean and see the skyline), don't really mean a hill of beans. We'd better start enjoying each and every moment we have here. Savor the moments; smile, laugh, and stop worrying so much. That is what I get out of looking up at the stars or out at the ocean.

It sounds weird. Sounds totally contradictory...but realizing one's insignificance can actually make you feel better about yourself, and help you to enjoy your brief time on this land of vastness we call earth even more.

Simple Character Test
Part 1

Want a quick test into the character of a person?

Under the heading of Little Things Can Be So Telling About Someone. Observe this, and tell me it is not a window into a person's larger self.

Watch an individual when you are on an airplane and it is time to rest and put the seat back.

We see basically two types of folks.

There are some who just belly up to the bar, push that recline button in as hard as they can, lean back, and head into comfy-comfy land—with absolutely no clue or concern for the comfort of the already legroom-deprived passenger behind them.

The other type is the passenger who would like to lean back for some extra comfort, but does not because they know it will be uncomfortable for the person behind them—who, by the way, let's assume they do not even know.

This is such a small item. A really insignificant tick on the whole behavior meter. But boy, does it tell a lot about the type of person you are or whom you are dealing with and how they look at others (and themselves).

Simple Character Test
Part 2

Here is another small, but telling example...

Observe people talking on the issue of illegal immigration and border control, etc. No matter where you lie in the argument, no matter how far left or right you are, try this simple observation.

See which people during the course of the argument use the term *illegal aliens* or *illegals* as opposed to those who use the term *immigrants*.

Hearing people use the terms *alien* or *illegal* to describe another human being? Hmm. I will save paper here, hold back my anger, and just say it says a lot about the person who uses those terms to describe another human being. Again, regardless of which side of the debate you are on...

This one little use of terminology can be a semi-bright window into the soul and character of any particular person.

Miles of Smiles

"If you're old enough to know better,
you're probably too old to do it."
~George Burns

A great football coach has the vision to see, the faith to believe,
the courage to do, and Peyton Manning to play quarterback.

Our drinking team has a softball problem.

Someone suggested starting National Déjà Vu Day:
Wear the same clothing, go to the same place, do the same thing.
Actually we have this already. It's called Tuesday.

Watching a chicken crossing the road is beautiful.
It's like watching poultry in motion.

"I like to play blackjack, just 'cause I like sitting in a semicircle."
~Comedian Steven Wright

Here is a test to find out whether your mission in life is over.
If you're alive—it is not.

Question of the Day...
Week...
Month...
Year

If a book about great failures doesn't sell,
is it a success?

Sought After, Thought Afters

"What is more mortifying than to feel you've missed the plum,
for lack of courage to shake the tree?"
~Logan Pearsall Smith

"We don't need to increase our goods or possessions
nearly as much as we need to scale down our wants.
Not wanting something is as good as possessing it."
~Donald Horban

"Knowledge speaks, but wisdom listens."
~Jimi Hendrix

"Peace of mind is attained,
not by ignoring problems, but by solving them."
~Raymund Hull

Poverty is not natural.
It is man-made, and it can be overcome and eradicated by the actions
of human beings.
~Nelson Mandela

Reminder to those who think it is best to fight fire with fire:
A fireman usually uses a hose and water to put out a fire.

"If you can't feed one hundred people,
then feed just one."
~Mother Teresa

Top Old-Time TV Supporting Actors/Actresses

have always had a certain affinity for some of the classic characters who have played supporting roles in some of our favorite TV shows of all time. Their humor, style, wit, and wisdom can so often—even in a limited role—add so much to the enjoyment and quality of the show.

There are literally thousands to choose from. But we will take a crack at a few of our favorites. Let's build up the suspense by going in descending order.

#4) Miss Hathaway—*Beverly Hillbillies*. The friendly, perpetually frustrated Miss Hathaway served as a buffer between Jed and the gang and the mean Mr. Mooney, all while having a crush on Jethro. Played to perfection by the brilliant Nancy Culp.

#3) The voice of Carlton, the doorman in *The Mary Tyler Moore Show*. Hard to believe a voice on the intercom could steal the scene, but fans of MTM will tell you he did nearly every time. Lorenzo Music was the actor who voiced it, and I don't think we ever got to see his face. But we did catch occasional glimpses of his arms as he was opening the door for one of Mary's many friends or suitors.

#2) Schneider, the handyman or "building soop" from *One Day at a Time*. This too-confident, too-cool, always-in-the-know handyman, played to maximum hilt by Mr. Pat Harrington, was hilarious each and every time on-screen. Through all of his professed machismo, he protected those teenage girls like they were his own, and he never tried to hit on single mom Bonnie Franklin.

#1) My personal favorite? And you won't find him on most top-ten lists: Angel from *The Rockford Files*. Homeless, drifter, drug user, but well-connected and possessing a heart of gold, he always gave some unique clues and life advice to the sometimes interested James Rockford. The comic touch was perfect for the otherwise mostly serious *Rockford Files* show.

Again the options here are almost endless. Personal choice abounds. But I think we can all agree these small-role supporting character actors and actresses were invaluable to the shows on which they appeared.

Got some of your own? Email your nominations to our website at jcsportsandtees@aol.com, and we will see what responses we get and then publish them for all to see.

You Win Some, You Lose Some... But You Always Play the Game

When things are going badly, remember: Things are never quite as bad as they seem. And when things are going good, we tend to think we can set the cruise control and forget that things can change on a dime.

Here are some words and reminders for both ends of the "how are things going?" spectrum.

IF YOU ARE STRUGGLING:

How a man plays a game shows something of his character. How he loses…shows all of it.

There is no failure, only feedback.

You don't drown by falling in the water; you drown by staying there.

Failure is the condiment that gives success its flavor.

"I missed nine thousand shots in my career. I lost over three hundred games. There have been six times I have taken the game winning shot— and missed. I have failed over and over again…and that is why I succeed." ~Michael Jordan

If you are not big enough to lose, you are not big enough to win.

264

If at first you don't succeed—
you're running about average.

"I am not discouraged,
because every failed attempt is another step forward."
~Thomas Edison

ON THE OTHER HAND, IF THINGS ARE GOING WELL:

"If what you have done yesterday, still looks big to you today…
then you haven't done much today."
~Duke University basketball coach Mike Krzyzeweski

"Even if you are on the right track,
you will get run over if you just sit there."
~Will Rogers

"You have thousands of opportunities to keep quiet.
Use every one of them.

Holding the mile record doesn't make it any easier to run the mile in
the future.

I know of only one bird that talks—the parrot—
and it can't fly very high.

If you let your head get too big,
it will break your neck.

Ability may get you to the top,
but character will keep you there.

Every morning in Africa a gazelle wakes up.
It knows it must run faster than the fastest lion or it will be killed.
Every morning a lion wakes up.
It knows it must outrun the slowest gazelle or it will starve to death.
It doesn't matter whether you are the lion or the gazelle—
when the sun comes up, you'd better be running!

AND MY PERSONAL FAVORITE…

Remember, you may be on top of the heap…
but you're still a part of it.

Jon Cohn

Springtime Poem by Henry Gibson (We Think)

"Spring has sprung,
The grass is riz,
I wonder where
The birdies iz."

By Henry Gibson

(Source: The TV show *Laugh In*)

Ernie Banks and His "Joy of the Game"

During the writing of this book, one of the great sports legends of all time passed away—the splendid Ernie Banks.

At the time I was working at a basketball facility whose company name was Joy of the Game.

A couple of days after Ernie's passing, I gathered a group of middle-school basketball players together after a practice. After briefly talking about the session just completed, I decided to ask the boys whether they had heard Ernie Banks had died. They all said they had.

What came next, though, surprised me a bit.

I asked them, besides being a Hall of Fame baseball player, what else they had heard about Ernie Banks that made him so popular. Silence. I waited a bit. More silence, no hands raised.

I then asked the boys whether their parents had told them anything about Ernie Banks and why he was so special. More silence.

Finally, I asked them whether maybe they had read something about Ernie that made him so unique. As they say in the sports world…the silence was deafening.

Assuming this group of young men was symbolic of the generation of youngsters out there who may not fully appreciate what Ernie Banks stood for, I felt somewhat of a journalistic obligation to write the following open letter to any of our young readers who, God forbid, are taking an admittedly literary giant backward step by reading this particular STUFF book.

But to our young readers who may not remember…

I guess the best way to describe Ernie, and why he was so special, is to go back to the name of the facility I was coaching at—Joy of the Game.

That term, more than any other, was the best way to describe Ernie Banks. Pure, unadulterated Joy of the Game. He truly loved baseball. He loved being with his teammates. He loved and cherished the opportunity to play in front of fans. He loved competing. He even enjoyed the simplest of things, like the outdoors and the sunshine.

Maybe even more importantly, he had the Joy of the Game in everyday life, off the baseball field. He was nice to people he did not know. He befriended countless number of fans who simply came up to say hello. He had a smile and kind words for almost everyone he met.

He brought the Joy of the Game to life as well as baseball.

So, here is the message to young athletes: You may not be getting as much playing time as you would like, you may not be playing the position you think you would be best at. You may be upset at certain practice routines or scheduling conflicts. You may be frustrated your team is losing.

Sports seasons can be long, and frustration and tiredness can build.

All of this is understood, and these are perfectly legitimate emotions to feel.

But maybe we can learn a little bit about how the now dearly departed Ernie Banks looked at things and handled disappointment.

Remember, Ernie never played in a playoff game. He never once got to taste post-season baseball. He was on some teams that lost ninety or even a hundred games in a season. He had more than his share of losing seasons.

But through all that disappointment, Ernie Banks understood the beauty of the game. The joy of competing. He didn't take it for granted. He relished every moment. He never complained. He *always* had a smile on his face.

Even more importantly, he treated everyone, even opponents, with not only respect but outright friendliness and caring.

He spread his sunshine to others…and in return that "sunshine" was given back to him

Lesson learned.

Thanks, Ernie, for being the greatest. And for all your "Joy of the Game."

Questions to Ponder

If a policeman were to arrest a mime,
does he still have to remind him that
he has the right to remain silent?

When they ship Styrofoam,
what do they pack it in?

If the little black box is made to survive the plane crash
no matter what happens—
why don't they make the whole plane out of the same material
as the little black box!

If a store is open twenty-four hours a day…seven days a week…
every day of the year,
then why do they need locks on the doors?

Use 'Em or Lose 'Em

A quick shout-out to the makers and creators of the gift card—or what has become known today as the "lazy man's easy-buy gift."

Yes, for the paranoid, if not horrified "what should I get her for a present?" shoppers such as myself, gift cards have become the easy alternative to wandering aimlessly from store to store in some dreaded endlessly large shopping mall staggering around in some kind of retail-induced haze. If there is medicine you can take for this particular affliction—I sure haven't found it.

But the gift card truly has been a time-saver, if not a mental health preserver. It eases the pressures of selecting a gift that won't embarrass you as the gift-giver—and as an extra bonus—it actually gives the receiver something they can use!

But here is the catch…

Turnabout is fair play. Friends and family and assorted strangers, too, have discovered the beauty and ease of the gift card. And you, most likely, are receiving your fair share—assuming you have friends…or family…or strangers who care at least a little bit about you.

Yes, more and more now, each of us receives gift cards as a thank-you or for a particular activity we may have done or as a present for a certain holiday or occasion.

Here is the key, though. And again your friendly STUFF book is here for assistance.

Do not—repeat—*do not* be passive when it comes to gift cards. It is the use 'em or lose 'em philosophy here, folks. *You have to know where these gift cards are at all times or they will disappear!*

Here is what usually happens. Most people put them aside, and they will drift, sneakily but assuredly, from kitchen counter, to desk, to cubbyhole, to cabinet, and then conclude their evil lifespan by hiding under some papers in a drawer you never even look in anymore.

This is not by chance, folks. This is a well-thought-out conspiracy.

Gift cards are programmed to do this. I am convinced there is some "super microchip" secretly built into them that makes them quietly but effectively move to more obscure locations in your house or apartment.

Again, this is not by happenstance. I am convinced this gift card "relocation" is planned and premeditated.

Be afraid. Be very afraid.

The only solution: Keep those gift cards you have just received in plain and visible sight. Know where they are at all times. Once a week at least, take inventory and make sure none have gone AWOL.

And most importantly—use them. The only way to prevent the eventual disappearance of the meandering gift card is to actively and aggressively look for ways to use it. If it is a restaurant gift card, make plans to go—soon. If it is a retail store gift card of some kind—you don't want to spend money wastefully…but look for things you need to buy and try to get them from the stores you have the cards for.

As a last resort, you can do what every true-blooded American has learned to do: Regift! That's right, just put 'em in an envelope, write a nice note, and send them packing to another house to get lost or mysteriously disappear. Perfect solution. And it saves you additional shopping time. Almost everyone ends up happy.

As a final note: If anyone knows how to make a gift card–seeking drone that can enter a house and instantly track down where unused gift cards are located, call me. I have a business venture for you.

The Geranium on the Windowsill Just Died, But Teacher, You Went Right On

Funny how little things, which seem fairly insignificant at the time, can sometimes stay with you throughout your life.

The impact of longevity is sometimes stronger than the initial innocent thought.

For example: Junior year of college. First class as a transfer student to the College of Applied Life Studies—University of Illinois. Teacher—the veteran department head and longtime, longtime (not sure of what, but looking at her, she was definitely longtime) Dr. Marianne Trekell.

She passes out a short easy-to-read book called *The Geranium on the Windowsill Just Died, But Teacher, You Went Right On*. A simple book about a teacher teaching a group of young grade-schoolers. The young teacher in the story had a set and determined lesson plan each and every day. An organized and dedicated teacher, no doubt.

But one day the flowers on the classroom windowsill, which the young kids in the class had been nurturing all year long, suddenly wilted and died. In the middle of one of the teacher's lessons, one of the kids raised his hand to ask about the flowers and why they had died.

The teacher disregarded the question, as they were in the middle of a planned discussion and lesson on mathematics. She continued on with the lesson. The kids were left wondering about their beloved plant, which had wilted into oblivion.

The teacher completed the mathematics lesson and forgets to get back to the young girl's question.

The lesson of the book, and the one Dr. Trekell imparted to us on this very first day of class, was simple and so well-illustrated in this short picture book:

Don't be so wrapped up in the routine of life that you forget to observe and enjoy the many fascinating and interesting things that can happen on a daily basis.

Always be open and welcome to new and interesting things that may happen during your daily routine.

Nothing dramatic here. It was just a simple moment in time. I walked out of class not really moved or motivated by this particular lesson. But I did think about it some. And it did stick with me for some odd and unbeknownst reason.

Now, here it is, some thirty-eight years later—and I still remember the message. And it is one I periodically think of and remind myself of.

The strength of that message has grown with me over the years.

Life is full of routine—by necessity, in most cases. It is to some extent a fact of life. I think Maslow—he of the "hierarchy of needs"— said something about this. But never be so wrapped up in this routine that you don't allow yourself to take notice and even soak up the small moments that come each and every day during our lives.

Simple lesson from one of many, many classes I partook in over my splendidly mediocre academic career. Seemed like not much at the time.

But surprisingly, one I still think of today. And the message has got stronger.

What things happening to us today seem insignificant for the most part? Who knows, maybe we will still remember some thirty or forty years from now? Some small but powerful message can hit us at any time—sometimes when we least expect it. Keep your eyes and your mind open. You never know when these moments may come.

Thank you Dr Trekell for a lesson well learned.

I Was Country When Country Wasn't Cool

That is the name of a Barbara Mandrell song from the late seventies. Even in my youth, when rock and roll and the hippie craze was in its heyday, I was always a closet lover of good, old-fashioned country music. My eight tracks of Kenny Rogers, Loretta Lynn, Waylon Jennings, Barbara Mandrell, and Ronnie Millsap are no longer with us. But their memory remains. May they (the eight tracks, not the singers who are still alive!) rest in peace.

Whatever your taste in music, though, there can be no question as to which type of music has the best, most creative titles. Country music...hands-down!

A sampling:

1. "Get your tongue out of my mouth, 'cause I am kissing you good-bye"

2. "If I can't be number one in your life, then number two on you"

3. "She got the gold mine and all I got was the shaft"

4. "My wife ran off with my best friend, and I sure do miss him"

5. "She got the ring, and I got the finger"

6. "Mama get the hammer, there is a fly on Pap's head"

7. "I'm the only hell Mama ever raised"

8. "I changed her oil...she changed my life"

9. "Keep your biscuits in the oven, and your buns in the bed"

10. "She told me I can't have my Kate and Edith, too"

11. "You were only a splinter as I slid down the banister of life"

12. "Her teeth were stained...but her heart was pure"

13. "I still miss you, baby...but my aim is getting better"

14. "I'm so miserable without you—it's like having you here!"

15. "If the phone don't ring—it's me!"

16. "She was actin' single and was drinking doubles"

17. "I haven't gone to bed with anyone ugly, but I sure woken up with a few"

And my personal favorite—who could forget, "If you ever leave me...I'm going with you."

Laugh Trax

The children of Israel wandered around the desert for forty years.
You see, even in biblical times, men refused to stop and ask for directions.

A great prophet once said,
"Artificial intelligence sure beats real stupidity."

A great salesman is someone who can tell you to go to hell,
and you will actually look forward to going.

Atheism is a non-prophet organization.

Question? What is the symbol for 0 in Roman numerals?

"I gave my kid a BB gun for his birthday.
He bought me a sweatshirt with a bull's-eye on the back."
~Rodney Dangerfield

Beer does not make you fat. It makes you lean:
lean against the wall, lean against the table, lean against other people…

The shortest distance between two points is usually under
road construction.

Shedding the Wedding (Expenses)

just read that as of year-end 2015, the average cost for wedding expenses will be somewhere in the high-rent neighborhood of $31,000.

Just in case you are keeping track, that is higher than the average yearly salary of nearly 50 percent of Americans. A fairly easy connect-the-dots puzzle to see something is wrong here.

Some might argue the entire "wedding industry" is like a locomotive gone out of control. What started out as a nice, reasonably priced train ride along the engagement and marriage tracks has slowly but surely gone to the point of being completely out of control. One could argue, very soon, that it is going to crash into something large and unforgiving. Like a bank loan.

So, how do we kill this dangerous downhill slide? How do we get wedding ceremonies back from the financial abyss that has handcuffed, and in a ceremonial way, tortured many a father-in-law and mother-in-law across our fine land? Yes, they who have had the unforgiving job of putting their John Hancock on many of the expense checks?

First, it's like being in a psychologist's office. Before you can solve the problem, you have to admit there is one.

There is no question that collectively, with the entire planning process, we have created a wedding cake–size monster that has gone slightly out of control.

A myriad of wedding-associated faculties all add to the problem. Wedding planners, wedding invitations, wedding envelopes, wedding consultations, wedding showers, bachelor parties, bachelorette parties, wedding cakes, reservations for churches or synagogues, reception halls, rehearsal dinners, wedding night appetizers, dinner menu decisions, the open bar, wedding table flowers, wedding photographer, wedding videographer, wedding band, etc.

It truly has become a conglomerate of almost epic proportions.

Now, we fully understand the excitement and "specialness" of this once-in-a-lifetime event (a good time here to disregard the statistics on how many marriages actually last), and that everyone wants to make the moment "special." But I am convinced weddings can be done simpler, more tastefully, with just as much heart and sentiment—and most importantly, LESS EXPENSIVELY!

The ultimate goal, with all due respect to the well-meaning and hardworking ladies and men of the marital wedding planning field, would be to eliminate permanently the need for a "wedding planner." They should go away, just like the political lobbyist and the tax collector and consultants.

Here is the problem. When people have the position of planning a wedding as their full-time job, there inevitably is going to be too much thought, time, and money put into what should be a fairly simple and beautiful ceremony. They are going to want to "earn their keep," and they will suggest more and more things to add to the wedding. Slowly but surely, you get pulled in, and before you know it, you have so many things coming at you that you are crying for "weddingess interruptess."

Sorry, but instead of a professional full-time wedding planner, the actual "wedding planner" should simply be you or maybe Mom or Dad or some friend.

A nice simple ceremony, a few heartwarming speeches, an open bar, a little karaoke music, and a Dominick's or Mariano's–inspired food spread and you have the wedding of your dreams, with money left over to pay off your college debts.

Everybody lives happily married ever after...or at least 52.7 percent of you do!

Bottom line: Deep breaths, everyone. And bring weddings back to the nice, simple, yet special ceremonies they were meant to be.

Jon Cohn

Another Job Elimination

We've taken the STUFF ax to a few professions out there so far. To review, in a somewhat dilapidated and completely unprofessional way, we have called for the end to (among others) consultants, lobbyists, and the immediately aforementioned wedding planners. And now I am afraid we have to add yet one more to the lineup for our employment guillotine.

For lack of a better term, we will call them tax people. I don't know what you officially call them…tax auditors? Tax consultants? Tax professionals? Basically, we are talking about anyone whose full-time job is to help people with their taxes.

Nothing against them personally…and they currently do provide a valuable service, no doubt. It's just the feeling here that no one should have helping people pay taxes as their full-time job. Is this what our forefathers envisioned when they initially formed the taxation concept here in the States? Is there not something drastically wrong with our tax system when we require full-time people to help us pay our taxes properly?

Think about that concept for just a minute.

I would argue that is just not a good, productive use of a person's professional life. Wait tables? You are serving the public. Clean the parks? You are serving the public. Teach in a school? You are serving the public. Do research helping to find cures for particular diseases? You are helping the public.

This is what people's professions should be about. Making a living while providing a service to our community.

But should your sole purpose be to help someone figure out how much taxes they should be paying their government? No. That just doesn't pass the smell test.

Now, of course, in today's tax environment, it is certainly not the tax professionals' fault. They are needed for sure right now—and they absolutely provide a valuable service. Because the tax code is so complicated!

So the solution is quite easy: simplify, simplify, simplify!

Of course, the hard part is figuring out how to simplify the tax code. What ideas might there be out there that actually get into the specifics of suggested changes?

Sadly, I don't have time in these fine pages to create a solution. And it is against my nature to argue against something without coming up with a positive alternative (hopefully if you have pained yourself reading the book thus far, you will have seen that), but I must refrain from doing so in this instance.

I don't know the solution. I don't know all the facts and figures. I don't know all the details. But I am convinced, absolutely convinced, that it can and should be done.

To come up with a new and simplified way of taxing citizens, you will probably need some creative, outside-the-box thinkers—non-governmental people, non-tax people—to give you some fresh perspectives. We will have to find people who are not caught up in the budgetary minutia of financial and mathematical thinking.

Clear minds and creative thinking will be needed to provide a better alternative. But it can be done. Of this I am convinced.

I will be the first to volunteer to be on an exploratory committee for this wondrous venture. (Truth be told, I just want to be on any "exploratory committee." They always sound so cool, and no one knows what they actually do.) Perfect!

WAIT....Still One More Profession to Eliminate!

Sorry. We gots to put one more occupation on the chopping block.

I don't really understand what they do. I have known many people who do it, but I still do not know what they actually do.

I do know many of them seem to make a whole lot of money doing it.

I am talking about traders. At the stock exchange. Futures, options, wheat, corn? Again, I don't really get it.

But my question is, while they are making loads of money, are they providing a service to the community? Are they actually helping anybody? Maybe so—'cause again, I really do not understand what they do.

But what is the value to our everyday lives? If there were no traders, could we still have our same basic lifestyle?

Maybe not. Maybe I am way off here. All I know is, there is a lot of money being made, and I am not sure a single one of them has affected my life or anyone else's life in any meaningful way.

At any rate, even though I am pleading ignorance just a bit on this one, we call for the elimination of yet another profession. The traders. Sorry. But someone had to do it.

But look at the bright side. If we throw a party for all of our cancelled professions—wedding planners, consultants, lobbyists, tax professionals, and traders? All in the same room sharing a few cocktails? Wow. That's one helluva a party.

We're talking all-star level shenanigans here. Just imagine the thrilling conversations!

Roll out the open bar, bring in a few dancing girls, and let the good times roll!

The Link...to Think

Do not follow where the path may lead.
Go instead where there is no path, and leave a trail.

"A really good day is when you laugh, when you cry, and when you think.
You do those three things…and that's a pretty good day."
~Basketball Coach Jim Valvano

We didn't come this far
to only come this far.

"Each person born into this world has a right to everything he needs.
His right, however, is bound up with that of every other creature
that inhabits the earth.
And it is bound up with that of every other creature,
and gives him no license to grab everything he can
without allowing a share for others."
~Linda Hogan

On the plaines of hesitation
Lie the bones of bountless millions
Who upon victory laid down to rest
And in resting, died.

Peas or Beans, Thoroughbred or Donkey: Which One Are You?

*P*eas and beans are in a jar. Shake up the jar, and you will find the peas drop to the bottom and the beans rise to the top. Leaders are like beans. When things get all shook up, that is when they rise to the top. How do you react when things get "all shook up"?

Or better yet—

Think about the difference between the thoroughbred horse and the donkey. When the donkey is kicked or whipped, it just sits there. It sulks. It balks. It does not move. It stalls incessantly.

But what happens when the thoroughbred horse is kicked or whipped? It responds with all the speed and sinewy strength it can muster. It fights and powers on through the finish line.

So, when you are pushed or kicked, are you the donkey, or the thoroughbred?

Trouble on the "Dear Abby" Horizon

To: Not *Dear Abby*

I have been engaged for almost a year. I am to be married next month. My fiancée's mother is not only very attractive, but really great and understanding. She is putting the entire wedding together, and she invited me to her place to go over the invitation list because it had grown quite a bit, beyond what we expected it to be.

When I got to her place, we reviewed the list and trimmed it down to just under a hundred…then she really floored me!

She said that in a month I would be a married man, but before that happened, she wanted to have sex with me. Then she just stood up and walked toward her bedroom. On her way she said that I knew where the front door was if I wanted to leave.

I stood there for about five minutes and finally decided I knew exactly how to deal with the situation. I headed straight out the front door. Right there, leaning against my car was her husband, my father-in-law-to-be. He was smiling. He explained they just wanted to be sure I was a good kid and would be true to their little girl. I shook his hand, and he congratulated me on passing their little test.

Abby, here is my question: Should I tell my fiancée what her parents did, and that I thought their "little test" was asinine and insulting to my character? Or should I keep the whole thing to myself, including the fact that the reason I went out to the car was to get a condom?

My Top Six Songs of All Time

1. "Sugar, Sugar" by The Archie's. The ultimate bubble-gum song. Since I was a kid, every time—I mean, every time—I hear it, it puts me in a good mood and makes me feel better. What better reason do we need for a number-one song?

2. "Piano Man" by Billy Joel. This classic tells a story. It has melody, depth, feeling, and heart all built into one. Has anyone ever made a movie out of this song? If not, why not?

3. "My Life" by Billy Joel. Classic rebellion song. Played it over and over again on a solo post-college cross-country trip. Sweet memories, and every bit as good when you hear it today.

4. "Take It Easy" by The Eagles. My vote for best top-down, open-the-windows driving song. Too bad I don't have a convertible, and too bad that even if I did, the weather in Chicago rarely allows for "top down" driving. But either way, "Take It Easy" is a great cruising song.

5. "My Way" by Frank Sinatra. The ultimate "pump up" song for our parents' generation. Sinatra at his best—which says enough right there. Important: Get the message of this song *before* you find out you are dying.

6. "One Shining Moment." This Dave Barrett/Teddy Prendergast song is a great tune, but made classic

by its use wrapping up the March Madness tournament in college basketball. When that song comes on—after three weeks of emotion, thrills, and the tears of these college kids and fans—and the video highlights of the three weeks are shown? It always brings chills. Always. And they're the good kind of chills.

Mascot-on-Mascot Violence

There are few things more entertaining in this fine world upon which we live than the rare moment in time when two mascots get into a real fight. I am not talking the teasing or tussling that mascots may get into on a friendly, just-for-show basis—but instead when this teasing goes to the next level and the school mascots actually get into a real fight.

Oh, that's good stuff. It rarely happens, but when it does, it is crowd entertainment of the vintage variety.

A case in point would be what my two kids and I still consider one of our finest father-and-sons outings. It was at a Northwestern University football game, and my kids, then around seven and nine years of age, witnessed—and to this day still talk about—the fight right in front of us between Texas Christian University's Horned Frog and Northwestern's very own Willy the Wildcat.

Absolute classic. None of us can remember anything about the game, including who won. But the fight between the Horned Frog and Willie the Wildcat? The memories will last a lifetime.

Not to Be Outdone

Continuing with the mascot theme...I am eminently fascinated with this topic. Book two could be in the offing—*Mascot* STUFF *People Might Want to Know?*—because there have been so many great moments over time.

Those of us of certain ages can reminisce about some of the following:

1. Los Angeles manager Tommy Lasorda losing his temper, coming out of the dugout, and punching the Phamed Phillie Phanatic in the gut.

2. Rufus, the Ohio University Bobcat mascot, running out toward the band and viciously sucker punching Ohio State's unsuspecting mascot, Brutus the Buckeye. So wrong, but so great.

3. Stanford's famous Tree mascot being arrested for drunk driving. Can't make that stuff up. The Stanford "Tree" was famous for stirring up controversial incidents. Which probably explains the constant complaints of opposing teams' fans trying to urinate on the Tree mascot.

4. Who could forget the famed 1985 drug trials involving Pittsburgh's very own "Pirate Parrot" mascot?

And my personal favorite…

1. Pittsburgh Pirate slugger Randall Simon using his bat to take out the Italian sausage during one of the famous sausage races held between innings at Milwaukee Brewers games. An absolute classic.

To review, the sausage races are a Brewers' baseball game tradition. It is a race around the park between "Stosh," the Polish sausage; "Brett," the bratwurst; "Guido," the Italian sausage; and some dude in a hot dog outfit.

This particular four-mascot race was a classic. All four were neck and neck with the crowd going crazy as they came by the visiting Pirates' dugout. Simon, a big, burly dude, gets up on the dugout steps and seemingly, in an innocent, non-planned act of playing around, takes his bat and nails the Italian sausage right in the knees as he runs by.

"Down goes the sausage!" The hot dog then tripped over him and fell, as well. The Polish sausage saw what happened, and he stops to help as mass confusion breaks out in the stadium.

Meanwhile, unbeknownst to the crowd and the other mascots, "Brett" the bratwurst, sees his opening and sprint ahead of the rest to easily cross the finish line as the winner—with the Italian sausage back a ways, still writhing in pain.

Yelling, screaming, arguing all ensued as the crowd was going crazy.

Now, that's entertainment! And the ensuing lawsuit by the Italian sausage, claiming Randall Simon as the plaintiff, wasn't bad entertainment, either.

What better time than now to say that one of my bucket list items is to be a mascot for a day? As long as it isn't the Tree!

Arby's...Really?

J ust a quick thought...

Does anybody actually go to Arby's restaurants anymore? They are still open. The chain still exists. But I can't think of a single person I have talked to who has actually eaten at Arby's in the past, oh, say...ten years!

I am convinced the Arby's restaurants are conducting business other than that of a fast-food eatery.

It might be an off-track betting parlor...maybe a local politicians' illegal meeting place...maybe some kind of tax write-off...maybe, but hopefully not, a place for happy endings. Or maybe they were ahead of the times and provided "medicinal marijuana" as a public service before it was officially legalized. (I always wondered about those potato cakes back in the day.)

But something must be going on there besides delivering fast food. Myself and a few of my cohorts are convinced of this.

As a side note, when they opened some forty years ago those roast beef sandwiches were *really* good. They were new, fresh, interesting, and tasty. It was the place to go back then. But then they changed the meat. The processed roast beef meat of Arby's today? A sad commentary of where we were and where we have gone.

And those potato cakes (rectangular hash-brown crunch)? Absolute heaven. I was a longtime Arby's "potato cake" eater, until at a certain age I actually started paying attention to my cholesterol levels.

Shower Power

I may be a party of one here...but I am a self-admitted shower-head "elitist."

When looking at a hotel room, or apartment, or even when buying a house, most people will look at the neighborhood, the schools, the décor, the square footage, and the kitchen setup. Or they'll consider the number of bedrooms, the views, the furniture layout, the real estate taxes, etc.

Not me. My priorities lie elsewhere. My first look and first instinct is to check out the shower. In particular, the showerhead. For some unexplained reason, I am fanatical about this (any other closet showerhead freaks out there? Feel free to email me; maybe we can start a support group).

Specifically here are the key things the showerhead elitist is looking for:

1. First and foremost, shower pressure. This is key! A shower with light pressure, dribbling down over your shoulders, is depressingly unsatisfying.

2. The height of the showerhead. This is key also! If the water spray only hits you at mid-shoulder level, this is unacceptable! You know you are in trouble if you have to dip, dive, and dunk just to get the nice hot water on your neck, upper shoulders, and head. This constant dipping is distracting and will cause lower back problems sooner than later. Make sure the showerhead is nice and high!

3. Is there enough hot water? Also key. Even if the pressure is good and the height is good, it becomes insignificant if the hot water runs out too quickly. On a cold winter night or morning, a long, extended hot shower is key. If the hot water runs out too soon? Problems.

   Understand this is more a function of the water heater system, but that gets too complicated. For reasons of simplicity, we are holding the showerhead entirely responsible for this particular factor.

4. Breadth and depth of spray. Now we are getting into the showerhead elitist's technical specifications. Is the showerhead adjustable? Can you get the spray wide enough to cover all parts unknown...and at the same time, is it adjustable so you can centralize the spray for a little harder, more specific spray in an area of, say, potential soreness?

These things may seem silly and inconsequential. But to we (I am optimistically saying *we*, hoping there is one other person somewhere besides myself) showerhead "elitists," these are all crucial and significant elements.

Jon Cohn

To Ponder, Down Yonder

We have enough youth;
how about a fountain of smart?

The more people I meet,
the more I like my dog.

I don't suffer from insanity.
I enjoy every minute of it.

Time is the best teacher—
too bad it kills all of its students.

Sign seen in psychologist's office:
"I am out of my mind. Be back in five minutes."

"Would you please call me a cab?"
"Sure. You're a cab."

Too Much Stuff!

Not the book STUFF! (Please.)

But just the items we all have consumed over so many years. Put as simply as can be, most of us have and desire too many "things."

I wish I could remember the name of the charity. I have tried Googling it, but I cannot seem to find it. If they closed up, it is a shame because their idea was right on. It had a name something like "Half Your Closet." The basic idea of the charity is that most of us could go through our shelves, drawers, and closets at home and give half of it away—and we would not miss any of it in the least.

I think the same would hold true for other rooms in the house, like the garage, kitchen, basement, and family room.

Too much stuff, folks. Too much stuff!

This description of *frugality* by Elise Boulding in the *Bits and Pieces* magazine is maybe the best I have read on the topic:

"Frugality is one of the most beautiful and joyful words in the English language, and yet one that we are culturally cut off from understanding and enjoying. The consumption society has made us feel that happiness lies in having things, and has failed to teach us the happiness of not having things."

So true, Elise, so true.

So, when in doubt—pack it up. Give it away. Ship it out. You will rarely miss it, and hopefully it can be of help to somebody else.

The Final Item

J ust like at the start of the book, I ask the same question. In a periodical exposition such as this, with notes and paragraphs on a variety of topics, how do you pick one with which to end?

Much too difficult, and much too much pressure on any one particular item.

So, after much consultation with our crack STUFF research team (basically me, and whoever was within shouting distance), we came to only one possible conclusion.

We will let the end of this book, be the start of the next one! Book number two in the STUFF arsenal is going to be about sports. It figures to be titled *Sports STUFF People Might Want to Know...From Someone Who Maybe Should be Writing a Book After All.*

The first item is going to be about competition and how you view your opponents.

I love what Super Bowl-winning football coach Pete Carroll (a man who knows how to succeed and still make it fun) said about this in his book *Win Forever*:

"Once I understood we really are competing with ourselves, it changed my view of future opponents. Many people confuse opponent with enemy—but in my experience, that is extremely unproductive. My opponents are not my enemies. My opponents are the people who offer me the opportunity to succeed. The tougher my opponents, the more they present me with an opportunity to live up to my full potential and to play my best. From an extreme perspective, that is a reason to love them, not hate them. At the end of the day, that opponent is the person who makes you into the best competitor you can be."

That, my friends, is a different look at the competitive relationship from a coach, Pete Carroll, who has always done things in an unconventional, but usually successful way.

And with that…this chapter in STUFF history will come to a close.

Thanks so much for reading this book. It truly is much appreciated!

And, remember, any and all comments are encouraged and can be sent to jcsportsandtees@aol.com. Also, we will be using this email address to inform people of our STUFF website which is upcoming

Final Thoughts on the Endings and the End Quotes from STUFF

Remember, when all is said and done,
usually more is said than done.

"Crossing the finish line is not the real end,
but instead the beginning of yet another journey."
~Amtuotsww
(Stands for "Author Made this Up On the Spot While Writing")

And finally, whoever wrapped it all up and said it better than this:

"The end of THE END is the best place to begin THE END,
because if you read THE END from the beginning of the beginning
of THE END to the end of the end of THE END,
you will arrive at the end."
~Lemony Snicket

The End

Thank You and Acknowledgments

Especially to:

Windy City Publishers, for providing the guide through the journey of writing a first book (a move they probably now regret).

My voices of reason, who offered suggestions and editing on the book: my IRS guy (Independent Reading Specialist), Bill DuBois; professional editing specialist Janet Dooley; Copy editor extroidanaire Christy, and Dr. Ann Cohn (AKA the wife).

And finally, to:

All the little people we sometimes forget to mention:

Mickey Rooney, jockey Willie Shoemaker, baseball player Eddie Gaedel, actor Gary Coleman, actor Danny DeVito, and of course, mini-me Verne Troyer. Oh...and the little guy from *Fantasy Island*, too—don't want to forget him!

Peeking here...
At the Back of the Book

Readers: Please choose one from one of the two options below:

FOR THOSE WHO ARE JUST BROWSING THROUGH AND PEEKING HERE IN THE BACK—AND HAVEN'T BOUGHT THE BOOK YET!

Thank you for at least checking out this part of the book. I, too, have been a big fan of checking out the back of the book before actually deciding to read it. I usually look for any interesting quotes, and maybe a picture of the author, that might entice me to start reading. Unfortunately, I have been given expert advice from editors, and in particular family members and friends, that putting my picture back here will definitely not "entice" anyone to keep reading.

Despite this glaring omission, we hope you decide to give the book a try. We have put together a myriad of ideas, opinions, snippets, and observations that hopefully will entertain if not, God forbid, in some small way—enlighten. We keep things pretty light (most of the time) and certainly allow you the chance to jump around the pages and get a feel for what it has to offer.

If you do decide to buy the book and read it, we really do appreciate it...and don't forget the real excitement—when finished, you can then proceed down to item #2 below...

FOR THOSE WHO ACTUALLY READ THE BOOK:

Thank you, thank you, thank you! And more thank-yous.

It is truly appreciated that you took the time to read this book.

Hopefully, it was not too painful of an experience. A few people close to me have mentioned that reading this book could qualify for community service hours for those serving probationary time. I, of course, did not appreciate the sentiment—but, what the heck? Whatever it takes to get readers!

I will say, personally, that this book has been nothing short of a labor of love to write. For so many years I would drive around or be walking around, and ideas, such as the ones presented here, would just pop into my head. Simple observations, often. But ones I felt deeply about. Finally, at some point, I decided to write some of these down. It was hard remembering at times, and I did learn the beauty of the "Notes" app on my iPhone to help me remember.

Finally, we more than encourage you to respond to any of the segments included in the book, or just in general—the book *en toto*, to our home email address at jcsportsandtees@aol.com. We will do our best to respond back in kind. And through a coming website, we hope to make this book and its readers somewhat interactive.

Imagine the possibilities! My editors already did, and they weren't too thrilled about it, actually.

Finally, and with full sincerity, we do thank you for your readership, and so with full MBHS (if you don't know what that is…you should not be reading this part!). We wish everyone out there the best of everything in the many days to come.

And thank you again for reading some STUFF!

Made in the USA
Charleston, SC
11 April 2016